The Heart, Head, and Hands of a Servant Leader

The Heart, Head, and Hands of a Servant Leader

Unleashing Personal Greatness to Serve Others

Michael J. Stabile, PhD

Copyright © 2016 Michael J. Stabile, PhD
FutureNow Consulting, LLC

All rights reserved. No part of this publication may be reproduced, stored in a retrieval system, or transmitted in any form or by any means (electronic, mechanical, photocopying, recording, or otherwise) without the written permission of the publisher. Printed in the United States of America
ISBN-13: 9781535068215
ISBN-10: 1535068213

FutureNow Consulting, LLC

Unless otherwise indicated, Scripture quotations are taken from the *New Kings James Version*. ©1982 by Thomas Nelson, Inc. Used by permission. All rights reserved. Scripture quotations labeled AMP are taken from the *Amplified® Bible*, copyright ©1954, 1958, 1962, 1965, 1987 by the Lockman Foundation. Used by permission. Scripture quotations labeled NASB are taken from the *New American Standard Bible®*, copyright ©1960, 1962, 1963, 1971, 1973, 1975, 1977, 1988 by Lockman Foundation. Used by permission. Scripture quotations labeled Holy Bible, New International Version®, NIV®, ©1973, 1978, 1984 by the International Bible Society. Used by permission of Zondervan. All rights reserved.

Dedication

The following pages are dedicated to the reader who is willing to hear and see the power of living as a servant leader. *Leadership is more caught than taught,* and what we need desperately in the age we are living in is not more talk but more examples of those who walk their talk. This book aims to help you live and model a life of serving the world from your "sweet spot" of greatness and influencing others, one person at a time.

To my lovely bride, best friend, encourager, life partner, and adviser, Pam. You are a model and example of what it means to be a servant leader: an ordinary person who lives an extraordinary life of influence in the daily routines and circumstances of life. You have taught me what unconditional love is all about. You have opened my eyes to unconditional belief in the human heart and human potential. You have modeled unconditional mercy and forgiveness. *To you, I dedicate this book.* There is really no me without you. You have been and will continue to be my source of inspiration.

To the readers, my hope is that this book will not just be information to think about—I hope that it will touch your heart and be used to stimulate, inspire, and transform.

As always, to my Lord and King Jesus Christ, for His glory and honor!

Contents

	Acknowledgments ix
	Introduction xi
Part 1	**Why the Heart, Head, and Hands of a Servant Leader?** ... 1
Chapter 1	The Ultimate Model 3
Chapter 2	The Master's Assessment 6
Chapter 3	The Master's Heart 14
Part 2	**What are the Heart, Head, and Hands of a Servant Leader?** 21
Chapter 4	The Heart of a Servant Leader 23
Chapter 5	The Head of a Servant Leader 27
Chapter 6	The Hands of a Servant Leader 31
Part 3	**How do Servant Leaders Maximize the Heart, Head, and Hands?** 37
Chapter 7	Maximizing the Heart: "Greatness" 39
Chapter 8	The Heart of a Servant Leader: TRUTH Model ... 44
Chapter 9	The Heart of a Servant Leader: TRUTH Model— Teachable 49
Chapter 10	The Heart of a Servant Leader: TRUTH Model— Respect 56
Chapter 11	The Heart of a Servant Leader: TRUTH Model— Unselfish 65

Chapter 12 The Heart of a Servant Leader: TRUTH Model—
    Trustworthy 70
Chapter 13 The Heart of a Servant Leader: TRUTH Model—
    Honesty 77
Chapter 14 The Head of a Servant Leader: Renewing the Mind.....82
Chapter 15 The Head of a Servant Leader: HABIT Model—
    The Power of Habits 86
Chapter 16 The Head of a Servant Leader: HABIT Model—
    Attention: Key to Change 91
Chapter 17 The Head of a Servant Leader: HABIT Model
    Approach— Build Connection: Empathy 100
Chapter 18 The Head of a Servant Leader: HABIT Model—
    Inhibit: Negative Thinking Patterns................110
Chapter 19 The Head of a Servant Leader: HABIT Model—
    Train: The 4R Model Approach 120
Chapter 20 The Hands of a Servant Leader: Balancing Care and
    Candor 131
Chapter 21 The Hands of a Servant Leader: Engage in Healthy
    Conflict..142

Epilogue · 157
Endnotes · 161
References · 167
About the Author · 175

Acknowledgments

It is in the quiet reflective times that the delicate relationship between writer and words comes alive. But a book is never formed alone. It takes a team of people who are influential in shaping the thoughts you are now reading.

Pam, thank you for always believing in me, encouraging me, and making me laugh at myself. Thank you for helping me with my thoughts and guiding me in the process to find the best expression of words that reflect the heart of this work. I love my life with you, and I am blessed to be your husband.

Although she is now in the presence of the Lord, my heart felt thanks to Mrs. Martha Rumble, my fifth grade teacher, for being a servant leader extraordinaire. Mrs. Rumble was and is the best teacher I have ever encountered in all my years as a student, teacher and professor. Your words, *"I see greatness in you"* were deeply seeded in my heart to unleash my "sweet spot" to serve and make a difference in the world. Mrs. Rumble you are an example of a true servant leader who served her students; she influenced and developed our minds, hearts, and spirits.

Thank you to my clients who are part of servant leadership teams for your willingness and commitment to apply the principles and concepts contained in this book to your lives personally and professionally. You have been an inspiration and a constant source of encouragement to me. You have provided me the opportunity to explore and work with you as a "living laboratory." We have made and are making a difference and impact with these timeless, universal truths, which are being confirmed by recent research in neuroscience.

Thank you to my graduate and doctoral students at Xavier University, Cincinnati, who were so open and hungry to hear the heart, head, and hands of servant leadership. You encouraged me and gave me feedback that was essential to the writing of this book.

Thank you to the editorial team at CreateSpace. Your professional services and customer service are outstanding, and I know you have made this book better as a result.

INTRODUCTION

Why this book?

For over forty years, I have studied leadership both informally and formally. It has been a focus for me since my late teens. I have also had the privilege of speaking to people of all walks of life and professions over these years through my workshops, seminars, conferences, and training groups, as well as my experiences in teaching graduate courses.

My life's work is to help "draw out the deep water" of unique potential and purpose locked within each individual. Potential is like buried treasure: it is untapped power, unused strength, dormant ability, and unrealized success. Purpose is your original intent—that which you were born to do. As noted by Myles Munroe, author and leadership expert, *All human beings possess deep inside of them the leadership spirit; but only those who capture the spirit of leadership ever become truly effective leaders.*[1]

Over the years, I struggled with my own leadership journey and with the process of helping others on theirs. Something was missing, and the lack of that needed element was hindering me and others from breaking through and realizing our potential and purpose. **How could we tap into the leadership capacity that I knew existed in all of us?**

I had read hundreds of books, journal articles, and research papers on leadership; I had attended numerous seminars, conferences, and summits addressing leadership development. Yet I was puzzled by the fact that even with the wealth of information, principles, precepts, and programs on the subject of leadership, there was still a "missing link."

John Maxwell, an author, speaker, and leadership expert, says, "Everything rises and falls on leadership." In other words, nothing happens without leadership. Nothing changes without leadership. Nothing develops without leadership. Nothing improves without leadership. Nothing is corrected without leadership.

It is not that we do not have people occupying positions of leadership in our world. We have many leaders—but sadly, not much leadership. We see this in all realms: social, business, religious, political, education, and so forth. But what kind of world have all these leaders and their predecessors produced?

Genius is found in simplicity.

Over two thousand years ago, a young Jewish rabbi introduced a radical concept of leadership. His philosophy not only defied the understanding of leadership of His day, but it also challenges the leadership thinking of contemporary theorists and practitioners. Conventional thinking on leadership has its roots in the ancient Greek and Roman cultures, which basically defined leadership in terms of the following: *How many people do you control? If you are a leader, how many people work under you? How many people look to you? How many people worship you? How many people admire you? How many people are afraid of you? How many direct reports do you have? How many people are on your payroll?*

The philosophy of Jesus of Nazareth makes a distinctive paradigm shift: **to serve is to lead.** It is not a question of how many people serve you; it is a question of how many people you serve. His idea of leadership is based on completely different values—values that resonate with the human spirit and connect to the deepest part of every person.

THE HEART, HEAD, AND HANDS OF A SERVANT LEADER

Jesus answers the questions around what I called the **"missing link" of leadership**. A leader is first and foremost a servant of the people. Who, then, is a leader? Anyone and everyone who is willing to serve! How do you become a leader by serving? You serve your gift through your sphere of influence. Jesus refers to "whoever wants to be great," which means anyone. That takes leadership out of the hands of just a few, the elite, and puts it within the grasp of everyone. He is giving us the key to unlocking greatness; in essence, He is saying, "If you want to be great, I've got the secret!" When you find your unique gift, your "sweet spot," and you serve it to the world, you are a leader. Whatever your sweet-spot gift is, it is not for you to keep; it is for you to give away to the world. God created you and gave it to you to serve to the world. In serving yourself to the world, you become great by design and purpose.

I believe the human spirit is marked by an inherent desire to lead. Everyone wants to be a leader, but few have tapped into the unique and divinely inscribed "spirit" of leadership. However, when men and women understand and embrace their unique and God-given potential and purpose, it unleashes that "spirit" of potential and purpose. This book is a result of the study and subsequent application of these principles to my life and the lives of my students and clients.

As you read this, you might be thinking that this a "religious" work or that it sounds too "spiritual." You may also be wary of people who quote scripture and talk about Jesus Christ, and thus find yourself questioning whether you should continue reading. I certainly understand, and I don't want that to happen with this book. Therefore, I would like to begin with a few words on where I am coming from.

I have coined the term **ancient future** to refer to the application of timeless and universal truths to recent discoveries and continuing research in neuroscience. Successful people have certain realizations and/or awakenings that forever change and transform the courses of their lives and thinking. These realizations are essential to a healthy life and are both scientifically and spiritually backed. I have found that there are obvious correlations between science/research and scripture. Realizing that universal principles exist is only one step; the most important step is making real change that causes transformation. Therefore, my "heart" goal is to share with you foundational concepts about who you really are through principle and design.

The book is divided into three parts that answer three fundamental questions about the heart, head, and hands of a servant leader, as follows:

Part 1: Why the heart, head, and hands of a servant leader? Why do we need to heed the message of servant leadership? In Part 1, we examine the core of the message and the rediscovery of why servant leadership is part of the human DNA and essential to reaching your potential.

Part 2: What are the heart, head, and hands of a servant leader? What is essential to know about each of the components—*heart*, *head*, and *hands*—of a servant leader? In Part 2, we examine the key concepts that can help you find your "sweet spot" of greatness and unleash your potential and purpose.

Part 3: How do servant leaders maximize the heart, head, and hands? How can we progressively grow and thrive as servant leaders? In Part 3, we explore timeless principles that are scientifically and spiritually backed. This section is filled with practical applications, tools, and examples of how to cultivate the heart, head, and hands of being a servant leader. As the saying goes, "You cannot teach what you don't know, and you cannot lead where you are not willing to go."

In the following pages, join me on this journey of discovering and unleashing your unique leadership potential through the heart, head, and hands of a servant leader.

PART 1

Why the Heart, Head, and Hands of a Servant Leader?

CHAPTER 1

THE ULTIMATE MODEL

> *Then, all of a sudden, there was a light in the world, and a man from Galilee, saying, Render unto Caesar the things that are Caesar's unto God the things that are God's.*
> —BILL O'REILLY AND MARTIN DUGARD,
> *KILLING JESUS: A HISTORY*

The greatest and ultimate leadership model was born in an obscure and forgotten town in the hills of ancient Judea—a village that, according to archeological research, had only one street and eleven houses. With no record of having any type of formal education, this young man introduced His model of leadership to simple village people, those belonging to the lowest social strata at that time.

The town where Jesus was born was a colony of the Roman Empire, and He was thus a subject of the imperial power. His solution to the oppression of one of the most brutal governments in history was **servant leadership**. To the mind of the Roman world, the words *servant* and *leadership* together would be a paradox or an oxymoron, but the term fits the leadership concept that Jesus exemplified. In the Roman way of thinking, anyone who was not a Roman citizen was considered subhuman, second class, and disposable. Thus, human life was worth little. The life expectancy was less than forty years—and far less if you happened to anger the Roman authorities.

The emperors during this era were Augustus and Tiberius. Over time, Tiberius became a cruel, depraved, immoral murderer who would kill for his own pleasure. The great republic was on its spiral down into moral decay. Tiberius was known for ruling from his isolated mountain fortress on the island of Capri off the coast of mainland Italy. The Roman Empire was vast, but the rumors and stories of Tiberius's aberrant and violent behavior traveled along the roads built by the legions and along all of the shipping lanes between Rome and her many outposts. He murdered at will, killing entire families for any perceived error. He defiled even the youngest child and retaliated against any women who would not have him—even women of noble birth and marriage. Such was life in the empire; justice and nobility were scarce among the ruling class. The *Pax Romana* (Latin for "Roman Peace") was anything but peaceful for the colonies and the people of that era. Fear, oppression, control, slavery, and punishment were the fate of the conquered people of the empire.

> *There was oppression—for those who were not friends of Tiberius Caesar… what was man for but to serve Caesar?*
>
> *There was persecution of a man who dared think differently, or heard strange voice or read strange manuscripts. There was enslavement of men whose tribes came not from Rome, disdain for those who did not have the familiar visage. And most of all, there was contempt for human life. What, to the strong, was one man more or less in a crowded world?*
>
> *Then, all of a sudden, there was a light in the world, and a man from Galilee, saying, Render unto Caesar the things that are Caesar's unto God the things that are God's.*[2]

Rome didn't tolerate threats, and the Romans had learned and mastered the art of torture and persecution. Revolutionaries and troublemakers were dealt with using one of the harshest, cruelest, and most horrific methods ever devised by humankind: crucifixion. Crucifixion, Roman style, was not just a barbarous way to kill but also a process of mentally and physically destroying a victim. In 71 BC, a slave rebellion led by a rebel named Spartacus was finally quenched, and the remaining followers were crucified in a 240-mile line of crosses that stretched almost all the way from Naples to Rome.

The puppet kings and rulers of Judea adopted the strategy and philosophy of Rome, and to some extent, this was a matter of survival. They paid homage to Emperor Tiberius and Rome in direct violation of Jewish law. Herod the Great and Herod Antipas were corrupt, cruel, and driven by their love for luxury; they levied tax after tax to finance their own lavish lifestyles. Anyone who dared to defy these puppet kings would receive the Roman-style execution. **Fear, harassment, helplessness, and hopelessness** were overtaking the people of Judea.

The religious leaders of Judea—the Pharisees, Sadducees, and temple teachers—were self-proclaimed men of God who viewed the teaching of Jesus in a manner similar to the way Rome viewed an armed revolutionary. They saw His message as a threat to their spiritual authority, and they devised a plan for a quiet arrest and hasty execution. The high priest of that time, Caiaphas, saw Jesus as a dangerous threat. Caiaphas had amassed his wealth and power through temple taxes, profits from the moneychangers, and temple concessions for sacrificial lambs. He had learned how to work with and through the Roman governors, and especially the new appointee, Pontius Pilate. Caiaphas and his family also owned farms outside of Jerusalem, so He had a great deal more than just religious teachings at stake.

It was in this context that the Master Servant Leader emerged on the scene. His life, message, and impact were revolutionary to the thinking and mind-set of the time and a perceived threat to the leaders and authorities of His day. **What made His message so radical that the mighty powers of Rome and the religious leaders of His time were so threatened?** He had no infrastructure, no earthly government behind Him, and no corporation supporting Him. Yet His simple words either enthralled or enraged people of the first century, and they continue to do so today in the twenty-first century. So let me ask again, why was His message so radical and threatening to the ancient Roman world, and **why is it still so radical and threatening today?**

CHAPTER 2

THE MASTER'S ASSESSMENT

> *When [Jesus] saw the crowds, he had compassion on them, because they were harassed and helpless, like sheep without a shepherd.*
> MATTHEW 9:36 NIV

Harassed is defined in the Oxford Online dictionary as "a feeling or looking strained through having too many demands made on one, to disturb persistently; as with trouble or cares; bother continually; pester; persecute; to trouble by repeated attacks, incursion, etc." In other words, to be harassed is to be under the control of an involuntary influence or external force and have no internal peace. To be harassed is to be a victim of circumstances for which you have no means of resistance. Harassed people are trapped in a cycle of life in which they struggle to survive. They are internally stressed and feel **helpless and hopeless** that life can be different, get better, or even change.

This is the Master's assessment of the state of humanity over two thousand years ago. This assessment applies to the condition of humanity today because, fundamentally, contemporary society hasn't changed much. Even the economically privileged in most of the industrialized and technologically advanced nations are harassed.

In fact, we might even be more stressed in the twenty-first century as we try to multitask our way through the day to keep up with our cyber-driven culture—responding to our smartphones when we should be enjoying dinner with our families; checking our e-mail at home or answering our voice mail from the beach on vacation; using our laptops on the weekends to tap into the office computer to squeeze in more work when we are supposed to be relaxing and getting refreshed.

Consider this day in the life of a typical American: You rise early every morning to go to a job you hate or dislike and work twelve hours or more, feeling you're not appreciated, valued, or respected for the job you do. Your boss rarely takes the time to interact with you—only when he or she needs something or something is wrong. You can't wait to get off of work, only to be stuck in traffic again. At home, you eat unhealthy carryout dinners in front of the television's depressing news of crime, terrorism, and sleazy politics, and you watch a "reality" show that isn't real. Finally, you have to take sleeping pills to get some rest. Too often, you climb into bed exhausted, lying back to back with your spouse because either you're not speaking to each other or you're just so tired that talking takes too much effort. Six hours later, you wake up, still groggy, and start the whole thing over again. You get through the day hyped on overpriced and overcaffeinated coffee. You may continue in this manner until age 65 or 70, unless the company downsizes, moves overseas, or replaces you with someone younger who has no experience but will work for less pay. If you're lucky, you'll have a pension fund, social security, and health insurance to help in your postretirement years.

This is not life! What I just described is harassment, at least a modern form of it. When you are harassed, you are stressed internally; life is beating you up, and you feel helpless. You feel like you lack the capacity to generate change, and you live under circumstances that suppress your hope and suffocate your will.

Clearly, those living in the first century under the harassment of the Roman mind-set and rule faced a situation not much different than what we are facing today; the internal human conditions are still under harassment. Thus, the Master identified the cause of humanity's central problem. He didn't say it was sin or evil, although those are real issues.

Interestingly, He didn't give a "religious" description. He said it was the absence of effective and appropriate leadership. That's right, leadership! **Why did Jesus threaten the powers of His day and, for that matter, the powers of today?** He pointed out that their "leadership" led to harassment, hopelessness, and helplessness. On top of that, they were missing the original design for all human beings, and their selfish ambitions led only to destruction, moral decay, and despair. These were powerful reasons for Jesus to advocate change.

Let's examine the Master's assessment of the human condition. In the Gospel of Matthew 9:35–38 NIV, we find the following description:

> ***35** Jesus went through all the towns and villages, teaching in their synagogues, proclaiming the good news of the kingdom and healing every disease and sickness. **36** When he saw the crowds, he had compassion on them, because **they were harassed and helpless, like sheep without a shepherd**. **37** Then he said to his disciples, "The harvest is plentiful but the workers are few. **38** Ask the Lord of the harvest, therefore, to send out workers into his harvest field."*

Now we can unpack this assessment of the human condition. Jesus has spent time with the people of Judea, and as He travels through the towns and villages, teaching, healing, and serving people, He uses two words that, when properly understood, transform the perspective on leadership.

Harassed and Helpless

The first word is *harassed*; in the original language of the biblical writers, the word means to be under the control or involuntary influence of external forces—to have no internal peace. Harassed means that a person is a victim of circumstances for which he or she has no resistance. As Jesus observed people, He felt that they were trapped in a cycle of life, struggling to obtain the basics (food, water, clothing, shelter, and safety). In the Roman colonies, whether these needs would be met was always uncertain; the people were caught on a treadmill of so-called life. When you are harassed, life is beating you up, and you feel like you are always running after a runaway train.

Jesus saw people as living in a **harassed state of mind** and being beaten to a pulp, and He felt compassion for them and wanted to help.

The second word He used to describe humanity is *helpless*. In a state of helplessness, you lack the capacity to generate change and transformation. Helplessness means that you live under circumstances that imprison your hope and suffocate your personal will. This means you not only have problems, but you cannot seem to do anything about them. A helpless condition is a hopeless condition. When you have a paralysis of will and hope is deferred, a deep, dark hole of depression overcomes your being. All the dreams, ideas, desires, creativity, and innovation of the human spirit are quenched, and the exalted human being created in the image of God becomes just another lowly creature trying to survive on planet earth. In this condition, potential is minimized, and only base desires and needs become the priority. In the first century, people were powerless to drive away the occupying Romans or relieve their heavy taxation and persecution. They could not wish away their ills or diseases.

The Master identified the cause of humanity's central problem: they are "like sheep." Notice He doesn't say that they *are* sheep but that they are "like sheep without a shepherd." As with all of His statements, this is a concise, to-the-point pronouncement. Yet it embodies much more than the picture of a shepherd and his flock. To fully understand the scope of Jesus's word picture, it helps to understand the role of a shepherd and the nature of sheep. So I did some research on this relationship.

Sheep are single-minded, skittish, nearsighted, and highly social animals. They are best known for their strong flocking (herding) behavior and for following instinct. They will run from what frightens them and band together in large groups for protection. This is the only protection they have from predators. There is safety in numbers. They will become highly agitated if they are separated from the rest of the flock and are creatures of routine and habit. They are one of the few creatures that, if left on their own, will totally destroy their pasture. They are easily terrified and prone to wandering off from the flock. They require constant attention. They will continually repeat the process of wandering and getting into dangerous situations without ever learning to avoid them. Sheep have excellent hearing and recognize and respond to the voice of the shepherd. To minimize stress, the shepherd speaks to them in a quiet, calm voice.

Why do Sheep Need a Shepherd?
First, let's make this distinction: there is a difference between a hired hand and a shepherd. Throughout this discussion I use *he* and *him* to refer to the shepherd, but of course both men and women can be shepherds. A hired hand is motivated by compensation. A shepherd has a deep and committed interest in the sheep. By his own choice, he is responsible for what is not his. And his relationship is characterized by longevity and consistent presence, with or without significant compensation. The shepherd is at all times ready to lay down his life for the sheep. Sheep need a shepherd, because without one, they are vulnerable, self-destructive, and easy prey for predators. In Jesus's analogy of humans being like sheep, He is observing a shepherdless people who are vulnerable, self-destructive, and easy prey. He is really saying how much more a shepherd is needed for the people who are under the control

of "hired hands," those only motivated by their own prosperity, prestige, and power. People are a sacred trust, and serving them is an awesome commission.

Second, the shepherd recognizes that the sheep are not his to do with as he pleases. He understands that the sheep are not a tool, a means to an end, but a resource charged to his care. He is empowered, entrusted by another; he is responsible and answerable to one who has greater authority.

Third, the sheep hear, recognize, and follow the voice of their shepherd. The so-called leaders of the time were not concerned for the welfare of the masses, nor did they care about the plight of the common people. They did not have the trust or respect of the people, only their fear and contempt. Sheep, like people, naturally navigate to the familiar. Trust develops with experience gained in relationships. We have often heard that familiarity breeds contempt, but it also breeds trust, and with time and consistency, it strengthens expectations.

Fourth, the shepherd knows the sheep intimately and is able to call each by name. The leadership of the time saw people in numbers: censuses, taxes, and liabilities. There was no desire to know them personally and intimately. Shepherds use a system of sounds, clicks, and hisses to call the sheep, slightly different for each of the sheep in the flock, and every sheep knows and responds to the specific sound that is his or hers. Consistent, caring proximity is always recognized and always produces results. Relationship is the key: there is no such thing as an absentee shepherd. Connection is primary to the shepherd.

Fifth, the shepherd always leads the sheep into the safest, most beneficial conditions available and always away from harm. Strategically, he goes out before them, out of harm and into safety, always maintaining the lead. He never expects the sheep to move into circumstances he is not willing to withstand along with them; rather, he always expects more of himself than he does of those in his charge. What a contrast to the leaders of the day, who were doing the exact opposite; they were leading the people constantly into harm's way and, ultimately, destruction.

Last, the shepherd is willing to put the immediate needs and well-being of the sheep before his own, often at great personal risk. The well-being of those entrusted to him is paramount to the shepherd. This singularity of purpose encourages him always to ground his decisions in integrity. The shepherd is prepared to lay down his life, both literally and figuratively. Selfishness, self-promotion, ambition, pride, and so forth were the mind-set of the first-century leaders. Ultimately, they did nothing that put them at personal risk for the welfare of the people, concerning themselves only with their own.

The true shepherd understands the critical difference between power (often stolen and generally imposed oppressively upon the unsuspecting) and authority (which speaks of responsibility and answerability to a higher power).

The picture is a simple one, possibly too unsophisticated for the leaders of the Master's time or maybe even for those of today. But as we turn to the simple, we find that common sense, in its crystal clarity, is at its base. The Master's description was not "religious." He didn't say the problem was sin or evil; He stated that the cause of the mind-set of harassment and helplessness was the **lack of leadership**. Like sheep without a shepherd, the people had no leader! The leaders of that day, either by design or default, had failed the people. They had led them into a harassed and helpless state of mind, and like sheep, the people were wandering, headed straight for a dangerous cliff and certain destruction. The source of the people's condition was the absence or abuse of true leadership.

After identifying the problem, the Master presents the solution and gives his trainees directions, noting that there is plenty of work to be done but few workers on hand ready to do it. He tells his students that He is the Shepherd of the people who are like sheep, and they need to be the workers in the harvest among the harassed and helpless humanity in need of true leadership. The Master's lesson on servant leadership is to change the human condition and take the responsibility to break the chains of the harassed and helpless mind-set. It is an invitation to all, male and female, who wish to make not just a living but also a difference in the world.

CHAPTER 3

The Master's Heart

For as he thinks in his heart, so is he.
—Proverbs 23:7 NKJV

The idea of leadership that the Master proposed was countercultural to the thinking and lifestyle of His time; for that matter, it is still in opposition to our modern mind-set. In fact, Jesus was the ultimate example of what a leader was **not** supposed to be under the traditional philosophy. The Master's heart was really a reintroduction, helping us return to the knowledge of who we truly are as human beings by original design. His heart is that the potential and capacity for leadership is inherent in all people, not exclusive to some. This knowledge would change the world.

> *The majority of us think we are born followers, and by design, the "system" keeps most people followers. Our political systems and our governments, even democracies, reinforce the idea that few people will lead and others will follow. Every form of government in the world—whether it is Communism, Socialism, Democracy, or dictatorship—implies that leadership is reserved for a few, so we do not even aspire to be leaders. Education produces followers. Most people learn to become employees, not business owners. We have few classes now in trades or in entrepreneurship. Entrepreneurs would be leaders. Entrepreneurship begins when people discover that they have a gift*

and pursue their dreams. They start businesses and build the economy. They build strong nations.

Instead, our schools teach students to get jobs and work for someone else. Students learn to be a good employee. Most parents encourage this without realizing they are handicapping their children's potential. The whole system is set up this way, whether intentionally or by default.[3]

The rising popularity of the television program *Shark Tank* is a testimony to the innate desire for entrepreneurship, which is deeply embedded in the human spirit. *Shark Tank* is an American reality show that features a panel of business executives and investors (referred to as *sharks*) who consider offers and listen to pitches from entrepreneurs and small-business owners seeking funding for their businesses, products, or services. The critically acclaimed show has reinvigorated entrepreneurship in America and has also become a culturally defining series.

Speaker and author Dave Ramsey has been part of a movement of servant leaders who are empowering potential through an entrepreneurial focus. He has coined the word *EntreLeadership,* which is defined as "the process of leading to cause a venture to grow and prosper." EntreLeaders know how to blend their entrepreneurial passion with servant-like leadership that motivates employees through persuasion instead of intimidation. Here are just a few of his thoughts on leadership:

The very things you want from a leader are the very things the people you are leading expect from you. You must intentionally become more of each of these every day to grow yourself and your business. And to the extent you're not doing that, you're failing as a leader.

You want to know what is holding back your dreams from becoming a reality? Go look in your mirror. The good news is if you're the problem, you're also the solution.

How do you begin to foster and live out this spirit of serving your team with strength? Avoid executive perks and ivory towers. Eat lunch with your team in the company lunchroom every day. Get your own coffee sometimes. No reserved parking spots. Look for the little actions you can take that say to your team that while you are in charge, and while you lead from strength, you are all in this together.

Too many people in business have abandoned sight of the fact that their team members are humans they are people. Too many people in business have become so shallow that they are merely transactional, not relational. The people on your payroll are not units of production; they are people. They have dreams, goals, hurts, and crises. If you trample them or don't bother to engage them relationally you will forever struggle in your operations.[4]

Just as was true of the culture of Jesus's time, the culture of our time can destroy the mind-set necessary for the real you; it produces the thinking and philosophy that fit into what the power structure wants. That is why I have spent over thirty years fighting the pedagogy and curriculum structure of our educational system. The educational system has to a great extent become a hindrance to unleashing and unlocking the potential in each individual. The philosophy of the system becomes your way of thinking. Your system of thinking, your system of belief, begins with your thoughts. Average individuals do not tap into their potential primarily because of **self-doubt**. They lack the confidence in themselves to be leaders. When I discuss leadership, most people do not think I am talking about them. Some are convinced they have some leadership ability, but very few would call themselves leaders. Even those in roles of leadership, supervision, administration, and management often don't consider themselves to be leaders.

Solomon, one the wisest men who has ever lived, says that what you think determines who you are: "For as he thinks in his heart, so is he" (Proverbs 23:7 NKJV). The word we translate as *heart* in Solomon's statement is the Hebrew word meaning "the center of reasoning." This does not refer to the conscious mind but the "hidden mind." Psychology and neuroscience call it the subconscious mind. Whatever is stored in your subconscious mind is generally the "real" you.

The Master said, "Out of the abundance of the **heart** the mouth speaks" (Matthew 12:34 NKJV). What comes out of the heart can either be constructive or destructive, positive or negative. Jesus taught that the heart gives birth to actions. The actions are committed there, and then they come out in deeds. Your heart is where your mind-set and philosophy come from, and your ideas about life and leadership are shaped there.

What others think of us is important because we derive a large portion of our self-image from them, especially when we are young. That includes what our parents think and model, what our teachers think and model, what our peers think and model, and what our culture thinks and models. We can even internalize what those who have never met us think.

If you hear something and see it modeled often enough, you begin to believe it. Once you believe it, you react to life out of your belief system. If others tell you often enough and effectively enough that you cannot lead, you are likely to believe you cannot be a leader. We see through our mental frameworks and belief filters, not through our eyes. Your belief system and worldview are more powerful than sight. It has been shaped and formed, and you interpret what you see and hear through this filter. Words have power, and everything begins with thoughts and ideas—ideas control the world. The power of an idea is that it can create reality. To have an effect, ideas must be communicated from the mind of one person to the minds of others. It is words, either written or spoken, that transmit those ideas. The question for all of us to ask ourselves is this: **What words are in my heart, and how are they affecting my life?**

You can resist a self-limiting mind-set and belief system through a renewal process that transforms the heart and the way you think. The Master's heart message is simple and powerful: *I am the Shepherd, and everything, including you, was made by Me.*

The Master knew that every human being was created by design to be a leader in an area of gifting. His concept is for each person to be a leader among leaders. You may say to yourself, "I don't feel like a leader," or "I don't have a role or function as a leader." The question is **not whether** you are a leader, but **how** you are a leader. The commonly accepted system of thinking in the modern world has led us to believe the lies that lead directly to a *harassed and helpless mind-set*. Every human being was created with leadership potential, so we have a world of leaders. Each person in the Master's mind has a place or **"sweet spot"** where they come alive and can serve their gifts to the world. The original design of true leadership is becoming oneself for the benefit of others.

In uncovering and unleashing your leadership sweet spot, consider these **five principles** that I adapted from Dr. Myles Munroe's writings:

1. Every human being was created and designed to lead in his or her own "unique way."
2. Trapped inside the mentality of every follower is a hidden leader.
3. Every human being possesses leadership potential.
4. Leadership is your destiny.
5. We were born to lead, but each of us must take action to become a leader.

At the end of many of the chapters in this book, you will find questions to reflect on and steps for action prompted by the material. The first set follows.

Questions for Reflection

1. What is your leadership sweet spot?
2. What are you uniquely designed and assigned to be and do that only you can bring to the world?
3. Are you living by design or default?

Steps for Action

1. Take a personality or leadership assessment (e.g. The Leadership Potential Indictor [LPI], the DISC Personality Assessment, or the DEREK Leadership Assessment Profile [created by the author, for more information see www.futurenowed.com/assessments]).
2. Meet with an accountability person or mentor and probe your sweet spot with them.

PART 2

WHAT ARE THE HEART, HEAD, AND HANDS OF A SERVANT LEADER?

CHAPTER 4

THE HEART OF A SERVANT LEADER

The most valuable gift you have to offer is yourself.
—Bob Burg and John David Mann, *The Go-Giver*

To serve is to lead. The Master reintroduces the design: in order to lead, each must first become a servant. Servant leadership is not new, but it has been lost for so long that those who hear it today perceive it as new. In the 1970s, Robert Greenleaf, while working as an AT&T executive, conceptualized the notion of servant leadership and introduced it into the organizational context:

> *The Servant-Leader is servant first...It begins with the natural feeling that one wants to serve, to serve first. Then conscious choice brings one to aspire to lead...The best test, and difficult to administer is this: Do those served grow as persons? Do they, while being served, become healthier, wiser, freer, more autonomous, and more likely themselves to become servants? And, what is the effect on the least privileged in society? Will they benefit, or at least not further be harmed?*[5]

A distinguished list of authors, researchers, speakers, and organizational leaders from a variety of backgrounds and fields have embraced and embodied the heart message of servant leadership. Business leaders and authors such as James Autry, Ken Blanchard, Stephen Covey, Max De Pree, James Hunter, Herb Kelleher, John Miller, John Maxwell, James Sipe, and Larry Spears, just to name a few, have embraced and embodied the heart message of "to serve is to lead" in their lives, organizations, and writings. The works of researchers and theorists such as Peter Senge's *The Fifth Discipline*, Jim Collins's *Good to Great*, James Kouzes and Barry Posner's *The Leadership Challenge*, and Peter Block's *Stewardship: Choosing Service over Self-Interest* have noted empirical scientific evidence that correlates with the heart message of servant leadership.

A variety of organizations, such as Southwest Airlines, TD Industries, SAS, Wegmans Food Market, Nugget Market, Aflac, Zappos, REI, QuikTrip, Starbucks, Men's Warehouse, and Container Store, which have been mentioned in *Fortune* magazine's "100 Best Companies to Work For" are also companies that practice servant leadership:

> Fortune *magazine's annual list of the 100 Best Companies to Work For is out. It comes as no surprise that among the winners are many organizations from the list of servant leadership companies. What is especially noteworthy is that 5 of the top 10 Best Companies to Work For are also identified as companies practicing servant leadership.*[6]

Jesus's philosophy concerning leadership is important because societies' philosophies restricting leadership have not allowed leaders to emerge. Organizations, even the best-intentioned, have limited human potential, either consciously or unconsciously. Regardless of your perception, the heart message of servant leadership resonates deep within the human soul. Most have accepted the idea that they do not have the "right stuff" to be leaders. They have bought into an idea that is not true. Jesus came to reestablish the **"heart" plan**. He created us in His image to have dominion over the earth—for leadership—and that leadership is inherent in all of us. The Master reminds us that true leadership is service. Individuals and organizations that first recognize and then embrace this truth benefit and thrive. **Why? Because it is part of our human DNA.**

The heart of the Master is for us to unleash the key to personal success by discovering our personal giftings and assignments. We were each designed and conceived for an assignment. We were each born to lead in an area of gifting, and our attitudes toward life and leadership will be a product of discovering our gifts and our functions and serving them to the world.

You were born to lead, but you must become a leader. When you make the decision to cultivate your intrinsic leadership potential, a transformation will occur. Every human being has been endowed by the Creator with leadership potential in a unique and special area of gifting. However, it is only potential, and potential must first be discovered and then unleashed. True leadership begins with self-discovery and has very little to do with what you do; it is essentially a matter of becoming who you are. It is a choice and act of your will to be aligned with your unique design. It is the result of your commitment to self-manifestation. The truth is that you are a leader, regardless of your present status or your feelings about your leadership ability and potential.

Every product is designed by its manufacturer with the right parts and is engineered to accomplish the function that it was created to perform. When we talk of manufacturer settings or standard settings, these were part of the original design and are required to fulfill the manufacturer's intent. The same holds true for all of creation, including human beings. The Creator established the original design and purpose for humankind. He wired all humans with the capacity and natural ability to lead.

According to the Master, we are leaders by nature, and the way of leadership is to serve others. You may ask, **"What do I serve to others?"** Jesus's answer is simple. To become the great leader you were created and destined to become, you must discover your unique **"sweet spot"** or inherent gift and assignment, your purpose. True leadership is becoming a person who is valuable to others, rather than just a person of esteemed position or fame. If you find your unique sweet spot or special talent and commit to serving it to the world, then your significance will cause others to seek you out. When you are aligned in your sweet spot, you come alive. When you come alive, you will become a person of influence through exercising your gifts rather than through manipulation, position, or prestige. The more you become a person whose gift is valued, the greater your influence will be.

The shortest distance to leadership is service. This is why discovering your leadership sweet spot is a prerequisite to serving. What is in your heart is you; you are what you believe. You cannot live beyond the limits of your beliefs. In other words, your life is what you think it should be. Jesus, the ultimate leader of leaders, said that the truth will make us free. If the sources of our thoughts are not correct, then our thoughts are incorrect, and our conclusions and beliefs are defective or contaminated.

In the next chapter, we examine what constitutes the head, or mindset, of servant leaders.

CHAPTER 5

THE HEAD OF A SERVANT LEADER

> *And do not be conformed to this world, but be transformed by the renewing of your mind…*
> —Romans 12:2a NASB

"**Like sheep without a shepherd…**" The Master's assessment of humanity is summed up in these words. Not long ago, I lost electrical power during a thunderstorm. To top things off, I had forgotten to charge the battery on the computer, and I really needed to access my e-mail and send an important document to a client. I looked at the computer sitting on my desk and the cable box that enables access to the Internet; the power plugs were in the wall socket, and the physical casing of the computer and the cable box were present, with all of their parts intact. I also knew with reasonable certainty that the hardware and software had not been damaged. The only thing that was missing, which was preventing the computer's function and operation, was the electrical power flowing from the source. Everything the manufacturer had promised that the computer and the cable box could do was incapable of being fulfilled or experienced because there was no power.

This situation can be considered as an illustration of the picture that the Master summarizes regarding the state of the human condition. The heart of leadership exists deep down inside of each of us because we were designed by the Creator with this capacity, potential, and power. Yet we can't fully manifest this innate "sweet-spot" gift in our lives if we don't have the resources to access it. When this occurs, we have lost the "heart" of the Manufacturer's design, and we have lost our awareness of the mind-set that empowers us to exercise it effectively. Humanity's lack of connecting to this heart design has led to a loss of true leadership in the world. We have lost our power source.

Even though our potential as leaders is still within us in such cases, we've lost our connection with our Shepherd, our Source of purpose and power. Even if the connection is reinstated (the electricity), unless we have the right mechanism plugged into the power source—that is, unless we discover how a leader is to think and operate from his or her unique sweet spot—we still won't be able to fulfill our potential. It is our thinking that determines our lives. The greatest impact of this disconnect with the Shepherd is the mental damage of sheeplike behavior. As described in the discussion of sheep characteristics in Chapter 2, we become harassed and helpless—first in our thinking and then in our behaviors and actions.

It is our thinking that determines our lives. The greatest impact of this disconnect is a type of *mental damage* or *mental toxicity*. It is probably difficult to consider that many of our leaders, CEOs, political leaders, administrators, educators, celebrities, sports heroes, scientists, and lawmakers are suffering from a mental toxicity, but in light of what we are originally created to be, this is the reality that the Master describes to us.

When I use the term *mental toxicity*, I am not referring to a medical definition, people in an insane asylum, or people being psychologically incapable of sound judgment of what we call "normal" in our societies. What I am referring to is an inherent mental defect in every human being that has resulted from our detachment from our Creator/Manufacturer's design and purpose. I am referring to the confusion we all face with regard to discovering our identity, self-worth, self-image, self-esteem, and sense of destiny:

> *Men and women of every nation, race, culture, status, and socioeconomic context all seem to be doing everything imaginable to fulfill their deep*

internal desires to find purpose, significance, value, and self-worth. A study of our modern and postmodern societies will reveal that no matter how sophisticated we may believe we are; we are still haunted by a passion to know who we really are. Many have tried even destructive behaviors to make some sense of their lives.[7]

The result of this mental toxicity is self-hatred, self-denigration, self-deception (denying the truth about oneself, lying to one's self), fear (e.g., fear of failure, fear of success, fear of the unknown, a general suspicion of other people, a distrust of God), ignorance of personal identity, ignorance of personal ability, ignorance of personal purpose, ignorance of sense of destiny, and a mentality of survival (we don't really live—we just make a living).

Toxic thinking is like poison! A thought may seem to be harmless, but every thought counts. Every time you have a thought, it is actively changing your brain and your body—for better or worse. As noted by Caroline Leaf:

The surprising truth is that every single thought—whether it is positive or negative—goes through the same cycle when it forms. Thoughts are basically electrical impulses, chemicals, and neurons. They look like a tree with branches. As thoughts grow and become more permanent, more branches grow and connections become stronger...As you think, your thoughts are activated, which in turn activates your attitude, because your attitude is all of your thoughts put together and reflects you state of mind.[8]

We all have been experiencing the effects of our thoughts for our entire lives, yet we may not even know it! For example, have you ever become ill in the wake of a difficult or traumatic time in your life? You may not have made the connection, perhaps just chalking it up to "bad pizza" the night before or to coincidence, when it was more likely to have been the result of toxic thoughts taking their toll on your overall health.

The results of toxic thinking patterns translate into stress in your body, emotions, and spirit. Current research has confirmed that stress is more than just an emotion; it is a global term for extreme strain on your body's systems as a result of toxic thinking. It harms the body and mind in a multitude of ways, from patchy memory to severe mental health issues, immune system problems, heart problems, and digestive problems.

In Part 3 of this book, we will look more extensively at how to reverse the effects of negative thinking patterns and mind-sets by applying timeless principles with scientifically proven results. We can take control of our thinking and mind-sets. It is possible to control our thoughts and in turn unleash the power of our sweet-spot potential.

CHAPTER 6

THE HANDS OF A SERVANT LEADER

*Your true worth is determined by how much more
you give in value that you take in payment.*
—BOB BURG AND JOHN DAVID MANN, *THE GO-GIVER*

"*The harvest is plentiful, but the workers are few...*" The Master states plainly the condition of humankind and notes that there is an abundance of opportunity. The fields are ripe for harvest; however, there is a lack of true leadership. He makes clear by example and precept that humans are created to lead by serving themselves to the world from their unique design. You become a great leader when you serve your gift from your unique sweet spot.

Leadership is supposed to enhance, help, develop, and inspire others, not destroy, demean, and corrupt people. History is filled with examples of those who found their gifts but used them for their own personal ambitions, not for the advancement of the humanity.

Leadership, by design, is not for our personal benefit. It is for the advancement, progress, development, protection, and enhancement of others in the process of finding their own gifts to serve. A servant leader, according to the Master, is about salvaging humans, valuing them, and placing worth and equality foremost on humans. **Servant leaders are necessary for the world to become a better place, whether it is our personal world or the global community.**

MICHAEL J. STABILE, PHD

One of Dr. Myles Munroe's most repeated axioms is this: *"True leadership is self-discovery followed by self-manifestation."*[9] It is finding a personal, unique design and purpose and then serving and offering it to others. We first must learn and be aligned with who we are, and then reveal ourselves to the world. Greatness comes in serving to the world what we discover in ourselves.

Our world has a rich **"harvest"** of potential leaders. However, we must recognize and nurture the gifts in ourselves and in others. First, we must tap into our own potential and then help others achieve and maximize theirs. *If everyone was born to lead, why do so many demonstrate sheeplike characteristics and not live up to their potential?* There are probably many reasons, but as I have researched this, worked with leaders, assessed leadership potential, and personally coached leaders, I've found that **self-doubt** is at the top of the list.

When I work with leaders, I do an exercise called the *Frames of Heart Leadership Lifeline.* They are asked to look reflectively at all the people, events, and situations in their lives that they feel have had an influence on who they are as people and as leaders, both positively and negatively. Next, they construct a Leadership Lifeline of those people and events in a timeline format and use it to reflect upon patterns, lessons learned, or significant findings about themselves. This exercise came out of my own personal search and reflection undertaken to tap into what was hindering or interfering with my own personal growth, development, and potential.

As I created my Leadership Lifeline, I recognized a common theme that was a real blind spot and was holding me back from reaching my potential. At about the age of ten, **two very significant messages** were communicated to me. One message got engrained into my heart and soul, and the other I just didn't believe.

The first message was the one I just didn't believe, and it came from my fifth-grade teacher, Mrs. Rumble. Mrs. Rumble was and is the best teacher I have ever encountered in all my years as a student, teacher, and professor. In fact, I believe Mrs. Rumble was probably the favorite teacher of everyone who ever had her as a teacher. She was a rare combination of discipline and love. You always knew where you stood with her, but she treated every student with dignity and respect. You felt you were loved even when she was correcting you. One day, she asked me to stay after class and said she had something she needed to talk to me about. As you can imagine, I was a little apprehensive about meeting with Mrs. Rumble after school. Finally, the time came, and she sat me down and looked straight into my eyes and said these words: "Michael, I see you doing great things; you have greatness in you." I was just a chubby little kid and didn't believe I had much to offer, let alone greatness. By the way, at the time she said that to me, I had no idea what she meant, but I cherished these words in my heart.

The second message came from my dad at just about the same time. He was a fireman and worked twenty-four-hour shifts and then was off for forty-eight hours. It was early in the morning, and he had just come off duty and was having coffee with my mother at the kitchen table. They didn't know I was up and listening from the living room. Apparently, his buddies at the fire station were concerned about me, and I had been the topic of their conversations the day before. They were concerned that I was getting too fat and lazy, and they felt something had to be done to help me lose weight. Now I understand the circumstances that my father was facing, and his temperament was reactive. I don't remember everything that was said, but these words were inscribed on my heart and mind for years, leaving deep scars: "I am so ashamed of him, and I don't believe he will be able to amount to much." In my father's defense, he was venting to my mother and didn't intentionally try to hurt me. By the way, he never knew I heard those words; I held on to those in secret for many years. Those words were what I believed about myself well into my adult years; I carried them like a millstone tied around my neck.

As I looked at my Lifeline, it became clear to me that a pattern in my life was self-doubt, and now I could see the ugly roots that had grown out of a few words from a man I loved and admired. I had earned a football scholarship and had become the first in our family to go to college. I had a successful career as a teacher, coach, and principal. And yet I struggled with the pangs of self-doubt that were limiting my potential and chaining me down with a harassed and helpless mind-set.

It wasn't until I was in my late forties that I finally started embracing and living out the words that Mrs. Rumble spoke to me when I was a child. As you can glean from my story, I believed the words that my dad had said out of his own frustration and fears for my future, which ultimately led to fear and self-doubt. However, the words that Mrs. Rumble spoke were aligned to unleash my "sweet spot" to serve and make a difference in the world. Mrs. Rumble is an example of a true servant leader who served her students; she influenced and developed our minds, hearts, and spirits. When we overcome self-doubt and focus on self-discovery followed by self-manifestation, we do great things that influence others and, ultimately, the world. Thank you, Mrs. Rumble, for being a servant leader extraordinaire.

Servant leadership success is simple. It comes from an understanding of our value to others. It is only when we are convinced of our value that we are able to serve others willingly, eagerly, faithfully, and with integrity. Therefore, the key to leading is that you perceive your *sweet-spot* gifting as significant and valuable to others. You are significant if you have refined and developed your unique gift to the point that others will want it and know they can receive it if they come to you. You are the one they come to because they see that you are the only one who can meet that specific need. Whether it is a product or a service, you must demonstrate that it has been refined and is unique. What do you uniquely "bring to the table" that others need and want?

As you read this, you might be thinking, *What do you mean by "your unique and refined sweet-spot gift"?* If you are struggling with this question, as I did for years, then you are in good company. Researchers estimate that average individuals only tap into a very small percentage of their actual God-given potential in their lifetime. Some have stated that the average person only operates at **5 to 15 percent** of his or her potential. What if we could tap into more of that potential and maximize it to serve others and the world? I don't know about you, but I believe there would be a transformational revolution, and cultures would be transformed, one person at a time.

The image of the hands of a servant leader is about our actions and behavior that come out of our unique design and gifting. A true servant leader inspires others to become leaders and fulfill their purposes. In other words, true leadership success, according to the Master, is measured by diminishing the dependence of followers and the follower mentality. If our businesses, organizations, schools, families, churches, and governments would embrace the message of the Master, we would see people taking personal responsibility to solve problems, being less dependent on leaders, focusing on a greater good, looking for opportunities to serve others, and committing to causes much bigger than their own interests. The true measure of servant leaders is not how many people they lead, but how many of those they influence are leading as well—or at least are trained to lead.

In Part 3, we will unpack the following question: **How do servant leaders maximize their heart, head, and hands?** We do this through an exploration of how we can progressively grow and thrive as servant leaders and the scientifically and spiritually backed timeless principles that will help us in this journey.

PART 3

How do Servant Leaders Maximize the Heart, Head, and Hands?

CHAPTER 7

Maximizing the Heart: "Greatness"

> *Many people die with their music still in them. Why is this so? Too often it is because they are always getting ready to live. Before they know it, time runs out.*
> —Oliver Wendell Holmes

Speaking from my own personal experience, it is not easy to reverse years of **not** being trained to believe in yourself. When Mrs. Rumble spoke those words to me when I was a child, I didn't understand what she saw in me or what she meant by *greatness*. I thought greatness meant being famous, being a celebrity, becoming rich, being a sports star, or receiving some type of prestigious reward, such as the Nobel Peace Prize. What I have come to realize is that *greatness* is part of being created in the Creator's image. It is who we are as human beings. Greatness is separating yourself from the opinions others have of you. Greatness is freeing yourself from people's expectations. Greatness is discovering that you are more than what society or others think you are. The Master's class on servant leadership urges us to be **great**, which should be natural (Matthew 20:25–28):

> *Jesus called them together and said, You know that the rulers of the Gentiles lord it over them, and their high officials exercise authority over them. Not so with you, Instead **whoever wants to become great** among you must be your servant, and whoever wants to be first must be your*

slave; just as the son of man did not come to be served, but to serve, and to give his life a ransom for many.[10]

The Master doesn't tell His students that striving or desiring to be great is wrong; in fact, He acknowledges that it is natural to want greatness. That many shock you or seem in opposition to your image of Jesus. We many think that He was the opposite of that—that He was a humble, meek, and nice guy who wanted everybody just to turn the other cheek and shy away from any hint of self-promotion. In my experience, most of us were **taught the lie** that the Master said be kind to everyone and not desire to be great because that is opposite of true humility. The heart is the chamber that holds our convictions and values about all aspects of life. If we were taught to think from a place of weakness or to act like a doormat as the mark of humility, we would therefore act in a manner that reflects that way of thinking.

The root of the word *humility* is from the Latin *humilis,* meaning "low, lowly," from the Latin *humus,* meaning "ground." Some other word relatives are the Greek *khamai,* meaning "on the ground, human, kind, humane." So the progression begins with HUMus, earth; then becomes HUMble, lowly; and finally becomes HUMAN, Man. **In other words, to be humble means to be truly human by original design.** Humility, both the word and the concept, seems to be a paradox. It means the quality or condition of being humble; however, in contrast, the attribute of humility is highly praised. *Humble people are advanced people. Humble people are great!*

Instead of cowering or groveling, I picture the humble person as standing naked and not ashamed. The humble one is not naked in a physical or sexual sense but in the context of being one's real self, withholding nothing from him- or herself, from God, and from fellow humans, all of whom need to see the total truth. **The humble person has not the least taint of phoniness and stands straight in the naked truth, in honesty.**

Jesus says, "**Whoever wants to be great.**" As noted earlier, that means anyone, taking it out of the hands of just a few, the elite; it is within the grasp of everyone. He is giving us the key to unlocking greatness. In essence, He is saying, "If you want to be great, I've got the secret!" You don't control people, you don't manipulate people, you don't oppress people, you don't threaten people, and you don't use people for your own purposes. You first and foremost serve yourself to the people. Whoever wants to be the first one people look for when they want something done has to be the slave of his or her gift and unique sweet spot. He urges us to achieve greatness through the same heart that He modeled and demonstrated. Servant leadership is the discovery of one's unique purpose, gift, and talents and, once found, the unleashing of them in service to humankind. As noted by Dr. Myles Munroe,

> *The wealthiest place on earth is not the gold mines of South America or the diamond mines of South Africa. It is not the oil fields of Iran, Iraq, Kuwait, or the silver mines of Central America. The wealthiest place on earth is the cemetery. It holds the treasures that people never served humanity.*
>
> *It is wealthy because in the cemetery are books that were never written. In the graveyard is music that no one had a chance to hear, songs that were never sung! The graveyard is filled with magazines that were never published. The cemetery is filled with businesses that were never opened... visions that never became realities. The cemetery is filled with poetry that no one is every going to write. Films no one produced. Ministries no one started. Dream never pursued. Grants and scholarships for which none applied. The graveyard is filled with ideas that never were carried out, inventions that were never mass-produced, campaigns never run, and sermons never preached.*[11]

The heart of a servant leader is to aspire to be great, and the greatest will be the one who is the servant of all. Servant leaders serve everyone what they have because they are not waiting to become great; they are taking the advantage to serve at every opportunity. Servant leaders take responsibility to use their unique giftings and talents to serve, no matter how demeaning or trivial it may seem. If there is garbage on the floor, for example, that is an opportunity to demonstrate your gift for attention to detail and high standards to those in your family or organization. If someone is hurting, that is an opportunity to demonstrate your gift for empathizing and showing compassion to others. If there is a problem that needs to be tackled, that is an opportunity to take the lead by volunteering to head up a team to do it quickly. If you are in a gathering or meeting where no one is introducing themselves, *that* is an opportunity to serve by helping others to open up and connect.

The world's philosophy of greatness is dependent on how many people serve you. The Master's ideas of leadership are based on completely different values: **How many people do you serve?** Servant leadership is serving from you heart at every opportunity.

Our outward behavior and actions will reflect the inward conditions of our hearts. We become what we think. What we believe on the inside dictates what we are on the outside. Until we come to the point where our personal urgency level drives us to believe what is really true about us, nothing will change. Zig Ziglar, a popular speaker and writer, stated, "Your attitude, not your aptitude, will determine your altitude." Whatever personal limitations we place upon ourselves are a direct reflection of our beliefs about ourselves.

Human potential is limited because we may have a sheep's mentality or a harassed and helpless mind-set. We don't listen to or hear the inner voice of potential calling out from within us. Perception can become a person's reality. What makes servant leaders different is that they don't focus their attention on the interferences; instead, they focus on their potential to serve others. To a certain extent, they get over themselves and their own scars and focus on others. Servant leaders are ordinary people living their lives in extraordinary ways.

We all have to ask ourselves whether we are being paralyzed by our wrong perceptions and beliefs about ourselves. Do we hear an inner voice shaped by significant people? Have their words and actions been

barriers to our own personal growth and development? What is holding us back from greatness?

How do we cultivate and unlock our greatness to serve others? What are the values that can unleash the servant leader heart? In the next chapter, we will unpack the key heart principles of a servant leader, what I call the **TRUTH** principles.

CHAPTER 8

THE HEART OF A SERVANT LEADER: TRUTH MODEL

*Belief in the truth commences with the doubting
of all those "truths" we once believed.*
—FRIEDRICH NIETZSCHE

The heart of a servant leader is demonstrated by modeling **truth**. The Master said that the truth would set us free, but what is *truth*? Now this is not just a play on words, but truth really is at the core of a servant leader. What are the core characteristics that reflect the growing and thriving heart of a servant leader?

Dictionary.com defines the word *truth* as "the true or actual state of a matter; conformity with fact or reality; a verified or indisputable fact." Winston Churchill once stated, "Men occasionally stumble over the truth, but most of them pick themselves up and hurry off as if nothing had happened."

The Master saw true freedom as a result of understanding the **truth** about yourself and everyone else. In other words, no one can just give you the right to be truly free. Freedom is not something you must choose to receive; it is something that happens to you, and it is experienced. Truly free men and women can never be bound. They live it from the inside out.

The full concept of freedom is found in the very word itself. This word is constructed from the word *free* and the suffix *-dom*. **It is a state of being free.** The heart of servant leadership is a declaration of independence to leading yourself and others to be free from bondage to other people's opinions and prejudgments and to tap the unlimited personal potential and creatively serve it to the world. Any form of thinking, leadership, or system that restricts, denies, inhibits, limits, suppresses, oppresses, obstructs, or frustrates the God-given mandate and capacity is not leadership at all. **Our responsibility as servant leaders is to be truly free, and our mission is to set others free in our sphere of influence.**

Consider the following illustration of what I believe the Master is teaching us:

There is a reservoir in a valley which receives its supply from an inexhaustible reservoir on the mountain side. It is then true that the reservoir in the valley received its supply by virtue of the inflow of the water from the larger reservoir on the mountainside. It is also true that the water in this smaller reservoir is in nature, in quality, in characteristics identically the same as the larger reservoir that is its source. The difference, however, is this: the reservoir on the mountain side, in the amount of its water, so far transcends the reservoir in the valley that it can supply an innumerable number of like reservoirs and still be unexhausted.[12]

Here is the point: human beings were created by design to be like the reservoir in the valley. By nature, we are to reflect the nature, quality, and characteristics of the source reservoir, our Creator. However, the degree to which we open ourselves to this internal water supply will be the extent to which we tap into our greatness, our freedom, our potential, and our destiny.

Everyone was born to lead, but everyone must become that leader. It is a process of becoming a leader from the inside out. What are the character qualities that reflect the "reservoir source"? In other words, what are the characteristics that are ubiquitous to the heart of a servant leader?

Over the years, I have studied the character qualities of leaders, drawing from both ancient wisdom and modern neuroscience, and have found great agreement on those qualities. These attributes may be stated in different ways and given a variety of labels, but I have categorized and synthesized them in a model I call the **TRUTH principles**.

The Heart of a Servant Leader: TRUTH Principles

The TRUTH model identifies five key characteristics of the heart of a servant leader; these can be cultivated, developed, mentored, and coached. It is important to note that these characteristics are innate in all human beings, but for most, toxic thinking and mentality have contaminated them.

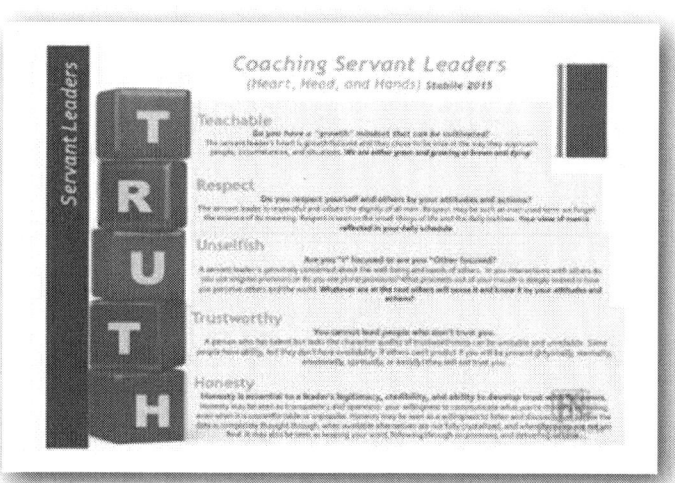

Let's briefly unpack the model here to give you an overview of each of the five characteristics; in the following chapters, we will dive deeper into each one.

Teachable
Do you have a "growth" or learner mind-set that can be cultivated? The servant leader's heart is growth-focused, and servant leaders choose to be wise in the way they approach people, circumstances, and situations. *We are either green and growing or brown and dying!*

Respect
Do you respect yourself and others, as shown by your attitudes and actions? The servant leader is respectful and values the dignity of all people. *Respect* may be such an overused term that we forget the essence of its meaning. Respect is seen in the small things of life and the daily routines. Your view of people is reflected in your daily schedule.

Unselfish
Are you "I" focused or "other" focused? A servant leader is genuinely concerned about the well-being and needs of others. In your interactions with others, do you use singular pronouns, or do you use plural pronouns? What comes out of your mouth is deeply seated in how you perceive others and the world. **Whatever is at the root, others will sense it and know it from your attitudes and actions.**

Trustworthy
You cannot lead people who don't trust you. A person who has talent but lacks the character quality of trustworthiness can be unstable and unreliable. *Some people have ability, but they don't have availability.* If others can't predict whether you will be present (physically, mentally, emotionally, spiritually, or socially), they will not trust you.

Honesty
Honesty is essential to a leader's legitimacy, credibility, and ability to develop trust with followers. Honesty may be seen as transparency and

openness—your willingness to communicate what you're thinking or feeling, even when it is uncomfortable or unpopular. Honesty may be seen as a willingness to listen and discuss issues before the data are completely thought through, when available alternatives are not fully crystallized, and when decisions are not yet final. It may also be seen as keeping your word, following through on promises, and delivering on time.

In the next chapters, we will explore and unpack each of the characteristics of the **TRUTH principles**. We will also use the model as a template and reflective tool for personal growth and coaching others in developing the **heart** of a servant leader.

CHAPTER 9

THE HEART OF A SERVANT LEADER: TRUTH MODEL—TEACHABLE

> *Give instruction to a wise man and he will be still wiser,*
> *Teach a righteous man and he will increase his learning.*
> —PROVERBS 9:9 NASB

Teachable

Do you have a "growth" or learner mind-set that can be cultivated? The servant leader's heart is growth-focused, and servant leaders choose to be wise in the way they approach people, circumstances, and situations. *We are either green and growing or brown and dying!*

What we know from ancient wisdom and modern science is that we have been designed for growth. Two things are fundamental for our survival as human beings: **protection and growth**. Both are controlled by your brain and nervous system. However, as Michael Fullan has written, "Change is inevitable, but growth is optional." We all have the fundamental capacity for growth and change, but we have to **choose** to grow. A teachable person, by an act of his or her will, chooses growth.

Carol Dweck is one of the world's leading researchers in the field of motivation; she is the Lewis and Virginia Eaton Professor of Psychology at Stanford University. Her research has focused on why people succeed and how to foster success. Her book *Mindset* conveys a simple idea gleaned from decades of research on achievement and success—a simple idea that makes all the difference:

> *What on earth would make someone a nonlearner? Everyone is born with an intense drive to learn. Infants stretch their skills daily. Not just ordinary skills, but the most difficult tasks of a lifetime, like learning to walk and talk. They never decide it's too hard or not worth the effort. Babies don't worry about making mistakes or humiliating themselves. They walk, they fall, and they get up. They just barge forward.*
>
> *In a growth mindset, people believe that their most basic abilities can be developed through dedication and hard work—brains and talent are just the starting point. This view creates a love of learning and a resilience that is essential for great accomplishment. Virtually all great people have had these qualities.*[13]

There is a principle stating that whenever someone shuts him- or herself off from the entrance of truth, learning, and ultimate growth because of fear, pride, preconceived opinions, prejudices, or any other reason, then truth, learning, and growth in their fullness will not come to that person from any source. On the other hand, if individuals open themselves up to truth, learning, and growth, they will see these flow from a variety sources and at every opportunity. **Thus, as the Master has said, *that* man or woman becomes free, whereas the other remains in bondage.** Wherever growth and learning are denied entrance and the rich blessings they carry, a person doesn't receive the deep roots of strength, power, and true wisdom they provide. When this is the case, the internal state of the individual will experience atrophy, toxic thinking, and the harassed and helpless mind-set the Master described.

In addition, not only do such individuals rob themselves of truth, growth, and learning, they **rob others** of contributions they could be making to set others free in an unfettered search for truth. When people close themselves off from being teachable, they are content with remaining in this position rather that endeavoring to achieve greatness in who they are and what they have been created to contribute. In other words, they become like **thieves and robbers**, self-focused, and the victims of their own thinking and mind-set, and they are content with this way of life.

The servant leader is the one who first and foremost is open to truth and is growing and thriving personally—but this is only the starting point. The servant leader's heart is to endeavor to bring others to a true knowledge of themselves and unleash them so that they are empowered to think differently and are equipped to come into their unique greatness.

In order to tap into your unique potential and unleash your personal greatness, you must be open and teachable. In my experience, all of the leaders I have talked with have agreed that **no one can really teach you how to be yourself, take charge, and express yourself—except you!** But there are some things that others have done or learned that are useful to think about in the process. Warren Bennis, a longtime leadership author and speaker, gives four lessons that I believe can be enlightening in developing a teachable growth mind-set:

1. **You are your own best teacher.**
2. **Accept responsibility. Blame no one.**
3. **You can learn anything you want to learn.**
4. **True understanding comes from reflecting on your experience.**[14]

Let's go into each of these lessons in more detail.

1. **You are your own best teacher.** Learning must be experienced as a personal transformation. A person doesn't gather learning as possessions but rather makes them part of him- or herself and becomes a new person. Bennis notes:

   Gib Akin, Professor at the McIntire School of Commerce, University of Virginia, studied the learning experiences of sixty managers. Writing for Organizational Dynamics, *Akin said that those he interviewed cited two basic motivations for*

> *learning. The first was a need to know, which they described as sometimes dominating their attention until satisfied. The second was "a sense of role" which stems from "a person's perception of the gap between what he or she is, and what he or she should be."*
>
> *In other words, the managers knew that they were not fulfilling their own potential, not expressing themselves fully.*[15]

In other words, these managers saw learning as something intimately connected with self. No one could have taught them this in school. They had to embrace and experience it themselves and, by choosing to act, teach themselves.

As an educator, I realize that knowledge is unique to each individual and that a person comes to know things best from connections through direct, personal exploration of the real world. The traditional and outdated understanding of learning and schooling has caused most of us not to embrace the idea that in order to learn, we must be willing to be personally responsive to and responsible for the learning. This axiom should be the foundation of a servant leader's thinking: **"You cannot teach what you do not know or lead where you are not willing to go."**

2. **Accept responsibility. Blame no one.** John Miller's popular books *QBQ and Flipping the Switch* emphasize the power of accepting responsibility! *The Question Behind the Question* provides a simple framework to practice personal accountability, both personally and professionally. It is a simple tool that helps us ask better questions and make better choices for ourselves by beginning with *What* or *How* rather than the *Why, When,* or *Who*. The spirit of *QBQ* is personal accountability, which is achieved by taking responsibility for yourself, your thinking, and your interactions. As Miller notes:

> *Why questions lead to complaining and victim thinking, as in, "Why is this happening to me?" When questions lead to procrastination, as in, "When are they going to get back to me?" Who*

questions lead to blame, as in "Who dropped the ball?" QBQs contain the word I, *not* they, them, you, *or even* we, *because I can change and only me. QBQs always focus on action.*[16]

Taking personal responsibility is about eliminating blame, complaining, and procrastination. When we play the blame game, what we are doing is delaying and hindering our own contributions while waiting for others to act; we are not taking ownership and putting personal responsibility into action. A servant leader is teachable when he or she steps up and is accountable to choose and take action to grow, learn, develop, and be open to others. A wise person takes ownership and doesn't wait for or look to others to take the first step.

3. **You can learn anything you want to learn.** This is one of the most basic tenets of learning. *You must have the wish, desire, and will to learn and grow.* A servant leader is passionate about the promises of life. The key to realizing these promises is a full deployment of yourself through choosing to learn and be a learner.

This kind of learning has to do with reflecting on experience and having an appetite for new experiences, recognizing that with these experiences comes adversity. In other words, you must be willing to step out of your comfort zone. Unless you have an appetite for absorbing new and potentially unsettling things, you don't learn. It is a kind of optimism and confidence that is not hindered by a fear of failure. It is a reframing of what it means to be a true learner. True learners expect and accept that there will be points of difficulty and struggles with any new experience. However, with struggle comes the natural process of learning. In essence, learning is a process of trial and error. It is a willingness to build on experience and develop the knowledge or skills to succeed. As John Maxwell has written is his popular book by the same name, we must learn to *fail forward.* Servant leaders are not afraid of failure, because they approach learning from a can-do perspective, not an "I can't" mindset. They have renewed their minds to learn how to look the possibility of failure in the eye confidently and move forward anyway. In life, the question is not whether you will have problems, but how you are going to deal with them. As Maxwell notes:

> *Successful people have learned to do what does not come naturally. Nothing worth achieving comes easily. The only way to fail forward and achieve your dreams is to cultivate tenacity and persistence...When it comes right down to it, I know of only one factor that separates those who consistently shine from those who don't: The difference between average people and achieving people is their perception of and response to failure. Nothing else has the same kind of impact on people's ability to achieve and to accomplish whatever their minds and hearts desire.*[17]

4. **True understanding comes from reflecting on your experience.** Reflecting on experience is one of the best ways to discover the truth about yourself and your life. The habit of reflection involves asking questions that provoke self-awareness. Nothing is truly yours until you understand it, own it, and progressively master it, and this includes your inner life and thoughts. **Clarity comes before action**, and if we are not self-aware, we just don't know how to act or even how to react, especially when it comes to our "raw" feelings.

Servant leaders practice reflection because reflective practice leads to understanding and wisdom. As Bennis notes:

> *Socrates said, "The unexamined life is not worth living." I'd go one step further: The unexamined life is impossible to live successfully. Like oarsmen, we generally move forward while looking backward, but not until we truly see the past—truly understand it—can we truly move forward and upward. Until you make your life your own, you're walking around in borrowed clothes. Leaders, whatever their field, are made up as much of their experiences as their skills, like everything else. Unlike everyone else, they use their experience rather than being used by it.*[18]

A servant leader is teachable, and he or she is progressively growing in self-knowledge, which leads to self-awareness, which in turn results in self-manifestation of personal greatness. We become great in our "sweet spot" because we have a teachable, self-directed heart to learn and grow.

Questions for Reflection

1. Are you and those you serve **teachable**?
2. Are you and those you serve "green and growing," and do they possess a growth mind-set?
3. Do you and those you serve **believe** that you can learn and grow and overcome any situation?
4. Do you and those you serve take **responsibility** for personal growth and development?
5. What is **hindering** you and those you serve from unleashing your personal greatness?

Steps for Action

1. What is one thing you can do **right now** to take charge of your learning and growth?
2. In your daily or weekly schedule, designate time for personal growth and development. Start out with small increments of time and then add to it as a habit develops (e.g. ten minutes a day or one hour a week).
3. Practice this new personal growth and development habit for at least thirty days.

CHAPTER 10

THE HEART OF A SERVANT LEADER: TRUTH MODEL—RESPECT

> *So in everything, do to others what you would have them do to you, for this sums up the Law and the Prophets.*
> —MATTHEW 7:12 NIV

As outlined in Chapter 1, the world of the Master, which was dominated by the philosophy of the Greeks and Romans, believed that leadership was a product of natural endowment, birth traits, and divine providence. The Roman Empire eventually disintegrated; however, its philosophies lived on as Europe grew and flourished. As the Europeans explored the Western world and spread their empires, the Greco-Roman philosophies dominated, and they still do so today. They form the basis of the thought paradigm of Western culture. One of those deeply embedded philosophies is the **value and respect** placed on human beings. The Greeks and Romans devalued anyone who was not a citizen of their cultures. As much as we don't want to admit it, we have some deeply rooted biases and prejudices toward other human beings, especially if they are very different from us. However, devaluing others is much more subtle in the modern era and can be seen in the way we treat others on a day-to-day basis.

Respect

Do you respect yourself and others by your attitudes and actions? The servant leader is respectful and values the dignity of all people. *Respect* may be such an overused term that we forget the essence of its meaning. Respect is seen in the small things of life and the daily routines. *Your view of people is reflected in your daily schedule.*

Relationships versus tasks. If your schedule is filled with tasks, things, projects, places to go, and so forth, it may indicate (1) that people and relationships are not your highest priority and (2) that relationships, although important, are not at the heart of how you operate. In fact, both research and my experience as a leadership coach and trainer indicate that most leaders have a **tasks-before-relationships mentality**.

Neuroscience and my own research have indicated that the higher a person moves up in terms of leadership/management responsibilities, the less empathetic and connected the individual becomes. The more task-focused you are or the more things that you are responsible for, the more you will become disconnected from, unaware of, insensitive to, or out of touch with the feelings and emotions of the other human beings you are in a position to lead or influence. The tasks cause atrophy in a part of the brain that makes us "other"-focused and aware. As noted by Daniel Goleman,

> *For leaders to get results, they need all three kinds of focus. Inner focus attunes us to our intuitions, guiding values and better decisions. Other focus smooths our connections to the people in our lives. And outer focus lets us navigate in the larger world. A leader tuned out of his internal world will be rudderless; one blind to the world of others will be clueless; those indifferent to the larger systems within which they operate will be blindsided.*[19]

The ability to work with people and develop relationships is absolutely indispensable to effective leadership. People truly do want to get along with people. **And although someone can have people skills and not be a**

good leader, an individual cannot be a good leader without people skills. Never underestimate the power of relationships in people's lives. If your relational skills are weak, your leadership will always suffer. As Maxwell puts it:

> *What does it take to have the focus required to be a truly effective leader? The keys are priorities and concentration. A leader who knows his or her priorities but lacks concentration knows what to do but never gets it done. If he or she has concentration but no priorities, he or she has excellence without progress. But when he or she harnesses both, he or she has the potential to achieve great things.*[20]

The power of connection. A servant leader makes connection with others a priority. In doing so, he or she elevates the trust levels and opens up the conversational space; most of all, he or she demonstrates respect and value of others in all actions. Leadership itself hinges on effectively capturing and directing the collective attention of others. **Leading with attention requires these elements:**

- **Focusing your own attention on what is most important "right now"**—this means a conscious awareness of what your priorities are in real time
- **Attracting and directing attention from others**—"People don't care how much you know until they know how much your care."
- **Getting and keeping the attention of employees, peers, family, friends, customers and clients**

A servant leader's ability to focus attention impacts the connection—the particular issues and goals he or she focuses on—guides the attention of those who follow him or her, whether or not the leader explicitly articulates his or her focus. People make their choices about where to focus based on their perception of what matters to the leader.

Listening to connect and discern, not reject and judge. How do you spell *respect*? People feel valued and respected when they feel like they have been truly listened to and heard without judgment. ***Are you a good***

listener? When was the last time you really paid close attention to people and what they have to say? Start listening not only for words, but also for feelings, meanings, and undercurrents.

To improve your listening, do the following:

- **Change your schedule.** Do you spend time listening to your family, followers, customers, competitors, and mentors? If you don't have all five groups on your calendar regularly, you're probably not giving them enough attention.
- **Meet people on their turf.** A key to being a good listener is to find common ground with people. Get to know who they are, and seek common ground to build your connections with them.
- **Listen between the lines.** As you interact with people, you certainly want to pay attention to the factual content of the conversation, but don't ignore the emotional content.
- **Follow the 70/30 principle.** A good guideline to facilitate balanced interaction that demonstrates respect and value is to **listen and ask questions 70 percent** of the time and **talk only 30 percent** of the time. Remember that servant leaders respect and value relationships, and the key is building trust by demonstrating this value and respect in your interactions.

When we talk more than we listen, others will default to feeling rejected, devalued, and judged. The way we communicate is key to bringing respect, and it begins with a shift in how we approach others. The power of connection starts with understanding, listening, truly hearing, asking "good" questions, and being open to another person's thoughts, opinions, and fears—and even to disagreements.

The success of your marriage, job, and personal relationships depends greatly on your ability to communicate. People will not follow you if they don't know what you want or where you are going. You can be a more effective communicator if you simplify your message and focus on the people with whom you're communicating. As you communicate, never forget that the goal of all communication is action. However,

clarity comes before action. If you dump a bunch of information on people, you're not communicating. Every time you speak to people, **first listen, then connect with understanding, then ask them open-ended questions, and then give them something to feel, something to remember, and something to do.**

Respect and value another's time. It is easy to forget that we are not the "center of the universe." The greatest lesson that Master taught us is that it isn't all about us. We demonstrate respect in how we value someone else's time. Probably the most valued asset all human beings possess is their time. You have probably heard this axiom: "The lack of planning on your part doesn't constitute an emergency on mine."

Psychologists say that not respecting the time of others is a serious sign of manipulation used to control others. People who are chronically late, or who seem to have no respect for the time of other people, are passively trying to control a situation with their tardiness. Those who don't respect the time of others, however, don't see it that way. They often have a narcissistic view that shouts, **"My time is more valuable than yours!"** This is rude, to say the least.

And far too often in personal relationships, this lack of respect is difficult to deal with. Most people operate on the assumption that a friend or family member is going to forgive them automatically for being late or, if something "comes up," for throwing a wrench in plans that have already been made. And yet, the fact that so many people are willing to do this to friends and family indicates a huge lack of respect for one another. I'm guilty; this is an area that I have really had to work on. I am on time and make it a priority not be late, except with my wife and family. It has been a struggle that I have had to work hard to reverse. When your family doesn't feel respected by you in what you say and the commitments you make, it causes relational damage and wounds that take a long time to heal. They feel devalued and lied to, and honestly, such issues tap into the family "trust" account. The truth is that as adults, it is vastly important to think about how others feel as well and not always operate under the preconceived notion that your life is busier, more important, or more hectic than someone else's.

One of the best quotes about respecting people's time is this:

> *We respect other people's time when we learn to value it as much as our own. Even better, we can get to a point where we won't distinguish between our time and the time of others.*[21]

In Craig Jarrow's "Time Management Ninja" blog, he shares the following **Ten Ways That You Are Wasting [Not Respecting] Other People's Time:**[22]

1. ***Calling when it should be an e-mail:*** *The modern cell phone is a technology marvel. Yet, being reachable anywhere and anytime has its limits. Ringing someone's phone is interrupting him or her. Don't ring that bell unless it is that important. Instead, consider an e-mail or another form of communication that can be addressed at the appropriate time.*
2. ***Interrupting:*** *Where else are you interrupting? If someone is working with the door shut or with headphones on, it probably isn't the right time to interrupt his or her productivity.*
3. ***Not respecting time boundaries:*** *I recently had a colleague text me at 4:22 a.m. That same day, he called me at 10:42 p.m. I am not sure what he had going on that day, but those two times were outside of my "time boundaries."*
4. ***Not doing what you say:*** *Broken promises affect not just your productivity but also those counting on you to deliver. Leaders can destroy the productivity of entire teams by their lack of follow-through.*
5. ***Spamming them:*** *Don't abuse others with your e-mail. If you are spamming others instead of doing work, then you are part of the problem.*
6. ***Not answering messages:*** *If you don't respond to others, you may be the communication bottleneck in the system. I know some leaders who are excellent in person, but they fail to answer any of their e-mail or other messages.*
7. ***Creating fire drills:*** *Do you create last-minute urgencies due to your disorganization? It isn't fair when your lack of action creates fire drills for*

others. Of course, if you are the one who constantly creates the fire drill, people eventually stop listening.
8. **Knocking twice:** *If you have sent someone an e-mail, you don't need to call the person to see if he or she got it. Or if you have called one of his or her phone numbers, you don't need to ring all the others. The individual is probably busy. Resist the urge to "knock twice."*
9. **Not being prepared for meetings:** *Do you show up to meetings unprepared? If you are not ready to discuss the issue at hand, then the session turns into a social gathering or a joint reading session.*
10. **Being late:** *Nothing disrespects another person's time like being late. At a recent business launch, the leader was 1.5 hours late. The entire launch team sat around for ninety minutes waiting on the boss.*

Here are few things to consider if you would like to **revise and refocus** the way you interact with others in demonstrating respect of time:

- **Be honest with yourself and stop overcommitting.** Respect your own time by being realistic in your plans for the day, week, month, and year.
- **Be mindful that you also are honoring others' time.** If you unintentionally don't honor someone's time, apologize profusely and work to amend the situation. If you dishonored someone's time and knew you were going to do so (deep down, you usually do), take some time out to figure out why you made that decision. Don't say, "Oh, it's because I'm a bad person," or "It's because I'm a procrastinator," or whatever guilt trip you like to put on yourself that allows you not to think about it. Do some real self-reflection and get your priorities straight.
- **When someone wants to meet or talk with you, make him or her give you a solid time and date.** I'll admit it: I stumble in this area. Because I'm so focused on what I have to do next or I'm too lazy to take the time, I'll give people the gray area—"Let's play it by ear" or "Let's get together soon"—and then we won't get together for weeks on end.
- **Do not allow people to pressure you to do something because they have an "emergency" or want to do something today.** Just

because it's an emergency for them doesn't mean it's an emergency for you, and just because it's convenient for them doesn't mean it's convenient for you. Realize that it's not OK for people to impose on your schedule.
- **Learn the power of the "no."** Often people give a low-quality no response, as in, "No—you're always bothering me," which isn't very helpful and puts you in a self-righteous, complaining mood. A high-quality no, on the other hand, has no negativity underneath what you're saying. It's simply a no, as in, "No, I won't be able to do that," or "No, my priorities won't allow me to do that." It's still a no, and people may still be mad, but you're coming from the right place when you say it.
- **Get comfortable with people being uncomfortable.** Yes, I'm using those words specifically because people will initially be furious with you when you start practicing this way of life, especially if you are a person who often said yes in the past. But remember, you are trying to have a purposeful life, make a difference in the world, and live in your "sweet spot." In order to do that, you have to get good at protecting yourself, and that is especially true of your time. *People don't have to like it; all they have to do is understand it.* And you can't be an excellent servant if you don't take care of your priorities first.

When we respect others and ourselves with our focus, attitude, actions, behavior, and time, we become better stewards of our unique "sweet spot," and that greatness begins to shine in the day-to-day routines of life. **Respect begins with you and influences all in your sphere of interactions.**

Questions for Reflection

1. What area or areas do you need to focus on in relationship to respecting yourself and others?
2. As you think and reflect on respect, what is the one area that needs the most improvement right now?
3. Do you and those you serve **show respect in the day-to-day routines of life**?

4. How would sharpening the focus on respect cause transformation for yourself and others?

Steps for Action

1. In your daily routines at work or at home, consciously remind yourself (on your calendar, smart phone, etc.) that your focus should be "Relationship over task." Make that phrase visible: post-it-note, screen saver, or in your notebook.
2. Practice being present by listening and asking questions.
3. As you practice respect through being present and listening, keep track of and notice differences in interactions and conversations for at least thirty days.

CHAPTER 11

THE HEART OF A SERVANT LEADER: TRUTH MODEL—UNSELFISH

> *Humility is not thinking less of yourself,*
> *it's thinking of yourself less.*
> —C. S. LEWIS

Although the terms *unselfish* and *selfless* can be used interchangeably, there is a difference. Being unselfish is simply not being selfish, which of course is a good thing if it leads you to be selfless. Being selfless means you will think more of others than yourself. The opening quote from C. S. Lewis holds true for **unselfish** leaders as well. Selfless is not a poor self-perception. To the contrary, being selfless requires a great deal of confidence. Being selfless does not mean running yourself ragged for a cause, either. Servant leaders must be healthy enough to deliver their service, and their teams should be as well. It is easy to get so caught up in our needs, our wants, our hurts, our failings, and ourselves that we become myopic. When we can't see past the immediate place we are in, we need to get outside ourselves and become selfless. We need to think less about ourselves and more about others. **How can we love our neighbors if we don't look up to see them?**

In the Greco-Roman thinking of the Western world that also dominated when the Master walked the earth, we see that **selflessness** has not been a highly celebrated attribute in leaders. Today's leaders are more often known for the size of their egos and the cults of personality that surround them. Many leaders spend their energies focusing on their personal rewards and status rather than focusing on the greater good of those they serve. Selflessness runs counter to human nature, which is why being *selfless* is so much more difficult than being *selfish*. It's natural to care about ourselves, and we are encouraged to think selfishly from all sides.

The Master was the most unselfish person who ever lived! In the book of Philippians, Paul gives us the definition of *unselfishness* that is deeply embedded in the heart of a servant leader following the way of the Master (Philippians 2:3–5 NASB):

Do nothing from selfishness or empty conceit, but with humility of mind let each of you regard one another as more important than himself; do not merely look out for your own personal interests, but also for the interests of others. Have this attitude in yourselves which was also in Christ Jesus.

So how do we become leaders who are more unselfish? The good news is that we don't have to sacrifice to a life-or-death degree—there is no need to die or spend years in prison for our cause. We also don't have to ignore our personal commitments and responsibilities. The bad news is that it still requires a great deal of work and personal sacrifice. The following are some simple lessons for those wishing to become more selfless, taken from Doug Moran's *If You Will Lead*:[23]

1. ***Subordinate our personal feelings/needs/ego to the greater good.*** *OK, this one is not simple. In fact, none of these lessons are easy, but when we commit ourselves to a cause, we will often need to put the cause ahead of our personal goals. This may mean sacrificing our pet project or sharing our strongest resources for the greater good of the organization or the team.*
2. **Selflessness takes practice.** *We can't just wake up one morning and become selfless leaders. It takes practice and discipline. Selflessness often goes against our natural instincts for self-preservation. It requires us to build and exercise new muscles. We have to look for opportunities, both big and small, to practice selflessness.*

3. ***Don't confuse selflessness with a lack of will or sense of self.*** Many may confuse selflessness with weakness or lack of will. On the contrary, selfless leaders often have huge egos and wills of iron. They know what they want. As leaders, we have to remember to keep thinking big and remaining confident, and we must know when and how to put the needs of our organization or cause first.
4. ***Selflessness requires leaders to understand boundaries and priorities.*** If the cause is great and we believe in our ability to effect change, we should be prepared to make equally great sacrifices. We may jeopardize a big promotion or bonus to do the right thing. We may even put our job on the line. We will also make smaller personal sacrifices, like missing family events or bringing the stress of work home with us. Selfless leadership requires us to explore our boundaries fully so that when we confront choices we are prepared to make them.

Greatness is found in being unselfish! Servant leaders facilitate the success of others. They spark action in others by seeing the value of others and aligning that value with the worthy cause. In the presence of great leadership, people feel inspired not only in the worthiness of the cause but also in their own personal worth. Great leadership makes others feel valued!

At this point, you might be thinking, "What are you talking about? How does one add more value by being unselfish and still survive?" When you focus on adding more value by being unselfish, two things happen. The first is that you virtually assure yourself of consistent and growing trust with others on all levels. Second, you make yourself more valuable to your team, organization, family, and others in your personal sphere. This doesn't happen because you're a nice person or because you deserve it or because you try really hard; it happens because you provide exceptional value to everyone around you, whether it is in your organization, your family, or another area of life. When you are selfless in your interactions, you provide a value that is observable, felt, and noticed.

In their best-selling book *The Go-Giver: A Little Story a Powerful Business Idea*, coauthors Bob Burg and John David Mann describe "go-givers" as those who add value to others in a way that helps them significantly while also personally increasing their sense of joy and personal and financial fulfillment. Go-givers are **other-focused instead of me-focused**.

The authors note that people who are successful in the long term, both financially and in their personal lives, are other-focused—"Your influence is determined by how abundantly you place other people's interest first"—and they go out of their way to add significant value to every relationship in which they are involved.[24]

The book chronicles the awakening of Joe, a hardworking but frustrated go-getter, and reveals **the five "laws" of stratospheric success**. Here is a summary of the five laws:[25]

The Law of Value: True worth is determined by "how much more you give in value than you take in payment." Strive to provide more in value—desirability to the end user—than what you charge (price).

The Law of Compensation: Income "is determined by how many people you serve and how well you serve them." The more lives you touch, the greater the compensation.

The Law of Influence: Influence is determined by how abundantly you place others' interests first. All things being equal, "people will do business with and refer business to those they know, like, and trust."

The Law of Authenticity: "The greatest gift you have to offer is yourself." People can tell when you are being truly genuine and not trying to be someone you are not.

The Law of Receptivity: "The key to effective giving is to stay open to receiving." Receiving is a natural result of giving.

Servant leaders always have confidence in their skills and abilities. They are comfortable in their own skins and know where they fit on a team or in an organization. But their actions are not driven by concern for self. They don't act based on how it will affect their own careers or whether it will make people like them. They don't worry about individual statistics. They act in the best interest of the **team** or **organization**. They put others before themselves.

Questions for Reflection

1. So how do you measure up—do you consistently put others first?
2. Do you measure your actions based on how they will make you look or what they will do for your own promotion?
3. Do you serve yourself or others?

Steps for Action

1. What is one thing you can do **right now** to put others first?
2. In your weekly schedule, designate time a time to send a personal note of encouragement to someone is your sphere of influence.
3. Once a week take someone out for lunch or coffee.

CHAPTER 12

The Heart of a Servant Leader: TRUTH Model—Trustworthy

Trust men and they will be true to you; treat them greatly and they will show themselves great.
—Ralph Waldo Emerson

Trust is the bedrock and foundation of influence. You cannot lead people who don't trust you. If people don't trust you, they will ignore you, resist you, and even sabotage your leadership. The question *Can I trust you?* is always on our minds whenever we interact with other people, particularly when we meet them for the first time, although we usually aren't consciously aware of asking it. Studies suggest that in order to figure out whether or not someone is trustworthy, we analyze the person's words and deeds to find answers to two questions: *Do you have good intentions toward me—are you a friend or a foe?* and *Do you have what it takes to act on those intentions?*

How would you define the word *trust*? *Webster's Dictionary* defines *trust* as **confidence in the honesty, integrity, reliability, and justice of another person.** Trust is one of the highest forms of human motivation. Being trustworthy is one of the hallmarks of a servant leader and reflects his or her inner life and character.

Trust, or lack of it, is the root of success or failure in all relationships, with spouses, family, friends, clients, colleagues, employees, employers, and organizations. In a climate of trust, people can work cooperatively to establish shared objectives and to seek reasonable ways of achieving them. Ironically, it usually requires many positive actions for us to earn and maintain others' trust, yet their confidence in us can be undermined if they perceive that even one of our actions is uncaring or self-serving.

In any economy, transactions between businesses and customers cannot occur without the exchange of some form of legitimate currency (money, goods, the promise of a percentage of profits, etc.). Likewise, servant leaders must have the **indispensable currency of trust** in order to enter into corporate agreements with their followers and/or members of their team. *Trust is like an account that people make deposits into on our behalf based on our character and behavior.* Without the currency of trust, we cannot function as servant leaders.

In his book *The Power of Character in Leadership*, Dr. Myles Munroe established some distinguishing marks of a servant leader in the process of character development:

The distinguishing mark of a leader is character. The distinguishing mark of character is trustworthiness. Trustworthiness is a product of stability established through testing over time…

A leader becomes trustworthy by staying consistent in character as he undergoes tests and trails over the course of time. Your trustworthiness is established when you have been tested over a long period—with such difficulties as changing circumstances, vocational challenges, personal crises, and temptations—and have either passed the tests or learned from them in the future.[26]

In other words, **there are no shortcuts to building a trustworthy character. It is a process.** Your trust as a leader is earned and maintained by the consistency you exhibit as you go through various tests over time. Therefore, an emerging leader must be tested to see if he or she can stand up under pressure. If you want to be trustworthy, you must learn that character is built through tests over time and that integrity involves the integration of your thoughts, words, and actions. With that said, leadership positions should not be given to people who have not yet been tested and tried. That is why, as servant leaders, we are to encourage, empower, and equip people by challenging them and putting them into situations that are out of their comfort zone.

We should not be quick to promote solely on potential and talent. The best and brightest may not necessarily be the most trustworthy. The trust account is sacred, and it cannot be expected. It must be earned. Who you are is more important that what you can do. The forging of character that is integrated with progressive consistency in words, actions, and attitude can only happen as we face situations and circumstances that reveal the substance of our hearts.

How can we build and sustain trust in our relationships with others? Of course, the answer is by being trustworthy. We can't have trust without being trustworthy. Trustworthiness, in turn, is based on ethical principles, including the principle of character (what we are as persons) and the principle of competence (what we are able to do as persons). For example, if you have faith in my character as a person but not in my competence as a leader, you may trust me as a friend, but you may not trust me to provide you with needed modeling, direction, and decisions of leadership. Alternatively, you might trust my intellectual and technical competence but lack confidence in my character.

So how do we find the answers? Decades of research and wisdom principles show that we are all highly tuned into the warmth and competence of those around us. Warmth is being friendly, kind, loyal, and empathetic. It is taken as evidence that you have good intentions toward others. Your competence—being thoughtful, creative, skilled, effective—is taken as evidence that you can act on your intentions if you want to.

Competent people are therefore valuable allies or potent enemies. Less competent people are objects of compassion or scorn.

The following **ten attributes of trustworthy people** are adapted from an article by Carl A. Osborne:[27]

1. *Because trust is based on truth, trustworthy people must be truthful.* Trustworthy people know that it's not enough to possess a truth; the truth must possess them. What is a common result when we learn that someone has lied to us? Whatever he or she says after that may be suspected of being false, however true it may be. Likewise, lies defended as white cannot always be easily dismissed. What we perceive as harmless or even beneficial may not be so in the eyes of the deceived.
2. *Trustworthy people are honest.* They match their words and feelings with their thoughts and actions. They do not think one thing and speak another. When we bad-mouth people behind their backs and sweet-talk them to their faces, we undermine trust. Trustworthy people do not take what belongs to others, whether it is ideas, statements, credit, or possessions, without their permission. They share successes by giving credit where credit is due. In addition to being honest themselves, trustworthy people strive to keep their associates honest by communication and constructive dialogue.
3. *Trustworthy people are reliable; they keep their promises.* Their "yes" means yes, and their "no" means no. They honor their commitments. This includes keeping appointments, whether they are with clients, colleagues, sales personnel, or family members. Few things inspire trust in another sooner than punctuality. You might as well steal another's money as their time.
4. *Trustworthy people are loyal.* They try to be especially loyal to those who are not present. By defending those who are absent, we retain and build the trust of those who are present. Trustworthy people know that to repeat unkind gossip about others is a divisive way of praising one's self. Therefore, they are careful not to repeat gossip unless they have a sound basis for considering it to be true and beneficial.
5. *Trustworthy people are not biased or prejudiced.* They strive to attribute good motives to the actions of other people. We are all prone to being too quick to censure others even though we do not endure advice ourselves.

> *Being quick to question the motives of others is not a sign of trust. We usually give ourselves credit for having good motives for what we say and do. Shouldn't we do the same for others?*

6. **Trustworthy people are humble, recognizing that the truth may not always be with them.** They interact with others on the assumption that they do not have all the answers and all the insights. They don't have a superior attitude. They value the viewpoints, judgments, and experiences of others. Therefore, trustworthy people try to understand others' viewpoints while maintaining their own commitment to proper values and principles. Having the inner strength to be humble, especially during times of provocation, is often the difference between those who command respect and those who demand it. Likewise, having a humble demeanor protects an individual from making damaging remarks and errors, thereby making advice easier to accept.

7. **Trustworthy people are accountable.** They try to recognize, admit, and accept responsibility for their own mistakes. If they say things they didn't intend to say, especially under times of stress, they are quick to apologize. They recognize that anger often gets them into trouble, but it is pride that keeps them there.

8. **Trustworthy people are cooperative.** They abide by the rules and policies of the organization. At the same time, they do not invalidate the spirit of the law by demanding the letter of the law. They know that just because they have the right to do it doesn't mean it's right to do it.

9. **Trustworthy people are just.** They are just not only to those who are just with them but also with those who endeavor to injure them. Trustworthy people strive to return kindness for offense and patience for impatience. They would rather suffer wrong than do wrong! They recognize that the best defense against misrepresentation is fine conduct.

10. **Trustworthy people promote communication and understanding.** They know that open and honest communication is built on the cement of trust. We can communicate with others we trust, almost without words. We even can make mistakes in our verbal communication and still find that they understand our true meaning.

When the level of trust is low, however, others may not believe even our most eloquent words. To foster trust, trustworthy people strive to share ideas and rationales for their positions and desires while maintaining genuine respect for others' ideas and perspectives. Why? Because they have learned that when trust is low, communication is exhausting, time-consuming, and often ineffective.

In summary, trustworthy people know that trust is gained more by conduct than just thoughts and words. Their daily conduct provides evidence of their intent to be honest, reliable, loyal, unbiased, humble, accountable, cooperative, just, and communicative. However, if trustworthiness is to grow, still more is required. Trust in others, in addition to our desire to be trusted by them, must motivate our conduct. **Trust is a two-way street.** To reach its greatest potential, it must allow interaction in two directions.

If we begin our relationships with individuals, organizations, or businesses with a lack of trust, then our relationships with them may not grow. Why? Without trust, there isn't a foundation to build permanent cooperation and collaboration. Likewise, if misunderstandings develop, there is little hope that distrusting individuals will work together to resolve their differences. Instead of talking directly with one another in this situation, it is common to tell our versions of misunderstandings to others in order to justify our positions. What is the antidote for a tendency not to trust others? The antidote is unselfishness. Our trust in others is a form of generosity. To paraphrase the golden rule, **shouldn't we strive to trust others as we would have them trust us?**

Questions for Reflection

1. What attribute or attributes are areas of strength for you?
2. What attribute or attributes need improvement?
3. Are you experiencing difficulties, trials, and testing? If so, how are you responding and what is your mind-set as you go through this time?
4. Is your life of inner thoughts consistent and congruent with your outer public life?

Steps for Action

1. Ask someone closest to you, whom you trust, about how trustworthy you are?
2. Identify one thing you can do right now in the area of being trustworthy.

CHAPTER 13

THE HEART OF A SERVANT LEADER: TRUTH MODEL—HONESTY

> *Whoever is careless with the truth in small matters*
> *cannot be trusted with important matters.*
> —ALBERT EINSTEIN

People want to follow leaders who place others' interests above their own. Servant leaders put other people's needs first. *The measure of success is whether those who are served grow—whether they become healthier, wiser, freer, more autonomous, and more capable—and whether they are likely to become servant leaders in their own right.* This is not the image you see on reality TV, but it is the way things have been designed to work in the real world and what makes human beings connect with one another. In today's world, an honest leader is becoming a very rare commodity. People will not voluntarily follow self-serving leaders whose goals are to enrich only themselves.

Before people are going to follow you—or any other leader—willingly, they need to know that you are *honest*. Before they are going to heed your advice, take your direction, accept your guidance, trust your judgment, agree to your recommendations, buy your products, support your ideas, and implement your strategies voluntarily, people expect that either consciously or subconsciously you will measure up to this basic but essential quality.

In 1983, Jim Kouzes and Barry Posner in their seminal work *The Leadership Challenge* presented the results of their research in which they analyzed thousands of personal best leadership experiences. The authors administered a questionnaire to more than seventy-five thousand people throughout the world, asking what qualities in a leader would inspire them to follow *willingly*. The results are striking for their consistency. **Four characteristics rose to the top of the list, receiving more than 60 percent of the votes over time and across many cultures.**

For people to willingly follow a leader, the leader must be:

1. *Honest*
2. *Forward-looking*
3. *Inspiring*
4. *Competent*

These four characteristics are intimately bound up with the *five practices of exemplary leadership*. For example, you cannot *model the way* without being honest. You can't *inspire a shared vision* without being forward-looking and inspiring. Being competent allows you to both *challenge the process* and *enable others to act*. Kouzes and Posner also noted the following:

> **Honesty** *rose to the top of the list and emerged as the single most important characteristic people look for in leaders. Whether people follow a leader into battle or into the boardroom, they insist that he or she be truthful, ethical, and principled. The terms* **"integrity"** *and* **"character"** *came up frequently as another way of saying that they're looking for honesty. Honesty is strongly tied to values and ethics. People inherently admire leaders who know where they stand on important principles and have confidence in their own beliefs.*[28]

People want to know your values and beliefs, what you really care about, and what keeps you awake at night. They want to know who most influenced you, the events that shaped your attitudes, and the experiences that prepared you for the job. They want to know what drives you, what makes you happy, and what ticks you off. They want to know what you're like as a person and why you want to be their leader. They want to understand your personal story. They want to know why they ought to be following you. In other words, **honest transparency builds credibility**. Kouzes and Posner further note:

> *Credibility is the foundation of leadership. People have to believe in their leaders before they will willingly follow them. Credibility is about how leaders earn the trust and confidence of their constituents. It's about what people demand of their leaders as a prerequisite to contributing their hearts and minds willingly to a common cause, and it's about the actions leaders must take in order to intensify their constituents' commitment.*[29]

Being honest requires courage because it makes us vulnerable and accountable. To avoid stepping on the feelings of others with our honesty also requires tact. Clearly, being truly honest involves more than just telling the truth in every situation, but for people of integrity, it is the only acceptable choice. When it comes to being honest, all of us have some room for improvement. Here are a few practical strategies, adapted from the web teaching series "Do You Have the Courage to Be Honest?" by Jonathan Wells, to help you fine-tune your efforts to develop the courage to be both honest and tactful:[30]

Five Ways to Become Even More Honest

> *Integrity is telling myself the truth. And honesty is telling the truth to other people.*
> —SPENCER JOHNSON

1. **Set the record straight.** *Are there times when you have been less than honest in the past? Having the courage to review your past offenses may cause some discomfort, but recognizing where you have tweaked the truth in the past can help you identify patterns and stop them from continuing.*
2. **Practice honesty in the little things.** *There is a tendency to think that it's OK to add a little harmless flare to the little things where nothing is at stake. The problem is, if we are dishonest in little things it will carry over*

into more meaningful areas. It is much better to develop honest habits in the areas that require less courage first so we can build up our integrity to face the more difficult challenges.

3. **Honestly emphasize the positive.** *Just because we are being honest doesn't mean that it's our job to point out the faults and shortcomings of others. If we focus on the positive, then our honest evaluation of people and situations can be both refreshing and encouraging.*
4. **Don't confuse preferences with reality.** *It is easy to color our view of reality based on our personal likes and dislikes. To be honest with others we need to recognize that our personal preferences don't change reality. They only change how we feel about certain things. Being honest doesn't mean that we are obligated to express every feeling we have on every subject.*
5. **It's OK to say nothing.** *If someone puts you on the spot and being forthright is not in anyone's best interest, what can you do? Have the courage to tell them that you would rather not say. This can be difficult when they press you for an opinion. Still, you have the right to speak or remain silent. This is especially useful if someone is trying to pull you into a pointless argument or when someone's feelings are on the line.*

Being honest may not always be the easiest or most convenient course, and that's why courage is required. But honesty is the course of integrity and creditability. Regardless of the prevalence of dishonesty in our world, we all have the freedom to choose to live by a higher standard. People of integrity will always recognize and appreciate your honesty and courage to the model the way.

> *To be persuasive we must be believable; to be believable we must be credible; to be credible we must be truthful.*
> —EDWARD R. MURROW

As a servant leader, the focus on and development of transparency and honesty are essential. People are tired of the cloak of deception that serves the selfish interests of the few while dragging down the many. We can all do our part by setting a good example through modeling the way and by having the courage to be truly honest with ourselves and with others.

Questions for Reflection

1. What do I need to do today to grow and expand my integrity and credibility in the area of honesty?
2. What have I rationalized over time that may be areas that affect how others view me?
3. Do I have an accountability partner or group to call me out in this area of honesty?

Step for Action

1. With an accountability partner, go over the five areas to become more honest listed in this chapter and ask them to honestly rate you in each area.
2. Identify one area that you need to focus on for at least thirty days and take actionable steps to address that area.
3. Give permission to your accountability partner to monitor your progress.

CHAPTER 14

The Head of a Servant Leader: Renewing the Mind

For as he thinks in his heart, so is he.
—Proverbs 23:7 AMP

The Master said, "But the things that proceed out the mouth come from the heart, and those defile the man" (Matthew 15:18 NASB). The reference to the heart here is what modern science would call the subconscious mind—the deep-seated inner thoughts and mind-set that direct your life. In other words, we are what we repeatedly do, and we do what is in our "hearts." Servant leadership is not just a series of "good" actions toward others; it is a set of habits of life or mind-set. Thus, the process of being a servant leader is a process that comes from the inside out. It is a choice of the will in each moment of each day. **What you think and how you think reflect your true heart.**

The mind-set of a servant leader intentionally and purposefully focuses his or her attention on **replacing "bad" habits with "good" habits.** In essence, we are the sum of our habits. In our day-to-day lives, habits can often be tough to build because there are plenty of distractions that can lead us off the "straight and narrow" and right back to our old ways.

Habits are the brain's own internal productivity drivers. Constantly striving for more efficiency, the brain quickly transforms as many tasks and behaviors as possible into habits so that we can do them without thinking, thus freeing up more brainpower to tackle new challenges. In general, this modus operandi of our minds leads to incredible benefits. But on occasion, it makes it seem nearly impossible to break bad habits—or integrate new ones—when we don't know what's happening inside of the heart or subconscious mind.

To alleviate some of those troubles, we can examine some timeless ancient principles that are aligned with research on the science of habit development; then we can practically unpack them into actionable steps that anyone can apply. The **HABIT model** is a framework that I have developed from my study of servant leadership and the neuroscience of leadership. Over the past decade, my study and work with clients, along with my teaching of graduate students regarding transformational change, have accelerated my interest in the science of thought, habit, and change, which recently has emerged more prominently in professional journals, as well as in popular writing in magazines, blogs, and business and leadership books.

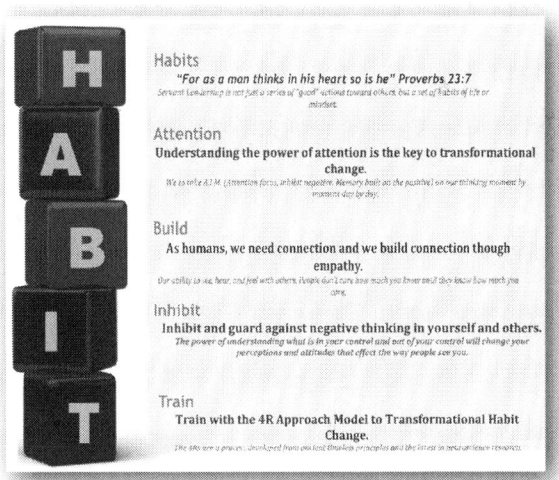

Here, we'll unpack an overview of the **HABIT model** framework and then expand on each component in the following chapters.

Habits

Servant leadership is not just a series of "good" actions toward others; it is a set of habits of life or mind-set. *Leadership is more caught than taught.* Your attitude, actions, and behaviors matter because your habits of heart are transmitted and can positively affect or inhibit the ways others see, hear, and understand you. If you are operating in a way that makes others unable to connect and feel valued, appreciated, and trusted, they will not be able to perform to their potential, which will create a toxic culture at home or work. Your habits are seated in your current mind-set and, good or bad, are being constantly translated to people around you.

Attention

Understanding the **power of attention** is the key to transformational change. We need to take **AIM** in our thinking moment-by-moment and day-by-day. Where we focus our attention determines what we see. Our focus becomes our reality. Attention is like a muscle: use it poorly and it atrophies; work it wisely and it grows. We will see how to take **AIM**, as Dr. Henry Cloud has coined it, at our habits and see them transformed and renewed.

Build

As humans, we need connection, and we **build connection through empathy.** Empathy is our ability to see, hear, and feel with others. People don't care how much you know until they feel and sense how much you care. Attention regulates emotion and the ability to be aware of self and others. The less self-aware you are, the larger is the gap in your ability to relate to and connect with others. Lack of self-awareness leaves you clueless to the real present needs of others. Caring builds on empathy, which in turn requires a focus on others.

Inhibit

Inhibit and **guard against negative thinking** in yourself and others. The power of understanding what is in your control and out your control will change your perception and attitudes, which will affect the way people see and perceive you. "We all need a daily checkup from the neck up to avoid stinkin' thinkin' which ultimately leads to hardening of the attitudes," notes Zig Ziglar. Don't get stuck in negative thinking patterns and mind-sets. The ability to spot negative thinking and effectively inhibit it from taking root is essential to a servant leadership mind-set.

Train

Train with the 4R approach to transformational habit change. The 4Rs approach is a process developed from ancient and timeless principles and the latest in neuroscience research. This approach will empower you with the knowledge and skills necessary to take charge of your life and future. The encouraging message for this process is that you do have control of your thinking and mind-set. **You can choose to change.** As this process evolved from research and practice over the last ten years, working with people from all walks of life, and even from different cultures, has been inspirational in my own journey.

I believe everyone can find freedom in their thought lives and mind-set, and because of this, I take complex ideas from neuroscience and bring them to life in an easy-to-understand way. In my own personal study, research, teaching, and leadership coaching practice, I see how there is alignment between the progressive research of neuroscience and ancient, timeless scriptural principles. You can overcome toxic thinking and its effects and, in turn, renew and refresh your mind. "As a man thinks in his heart, so is he." What you think about expands and grows, taking on a life of its own. The direction life takes can be either positive or negative; you get to choose. What you choose to think about can foster joy, peace, and happiness…or the complete opposite.

In the next chapters, we will explore and unpack each component of the **HABIT model** approach, using the model as a template and reflective tool for personal growth and for coaching others in the **head** of the servant leader.

CHAPTER 15

The Head of a Servant Leader: HABIT Model—The Power of Habits

All our life, so far as it has definite form, is but a mass of habits.
—William James

Most of the choices we make each day may feel like the complex products of sophisticated and well-considered decision-making, but in reality, they're not. They are habits. Each habit on its own means relatively little—such as brushing your teeth, taking a shower, putting the left or right sock on first, driving your car, what you say to family as you walk out the door, what you do first when you arrive at work, how and when you answer e-mail, how you organize your day, how you communicate to others, what you order for lunch, what you watch on TV, and so forth—until you realize that how you organize your thoughts at home and at work has a tremendous impact on your overall well-being. And that's not all: your habits of heart affect—both positively and negatively—all that you come in contact with.

Habits

Servant leadership is not just a series of "good" actions toward others; it is a set of habits of life or mind-set. *Leadership is more caught than taught.* Your attitude, actions, and behaviors matter, because your habits of heart are transmitted and positively affect or inhibit the ways others see, hear, and understand you. If you are operating in a way that makes others unable to connect with you or to feel valued, appreciated, and trusted by you, they will not be able to perform to their potential, which will create a toxic culture at home or work. Your habits are seated in your current mind-set and, good or bad, are being constantly translated to people around you.

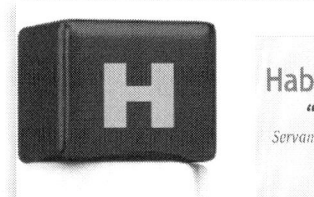

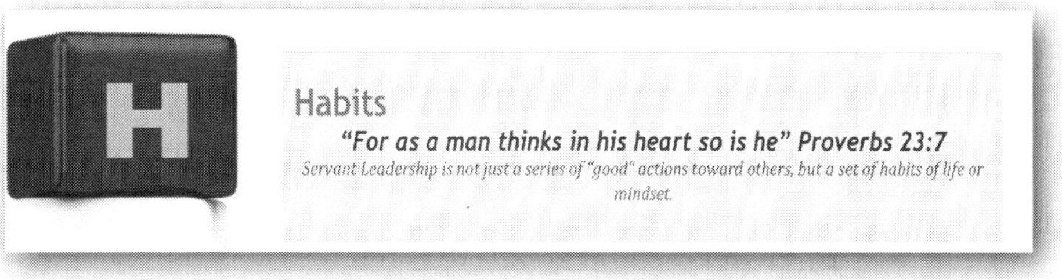

Habits
"For as a man thinks in his heart so is he" Proverbs 23:7
Servant Leadership is not just a series of "good" actions toward others, but a set of habits of life or mindset.

You may have been experiencing the effects of your thoughts and habits your entire life and may not have known it! For example, have you ever become ill in the wake of a difficult, traumatic, or anxious time in your life? You may not have made the connection, just chalking it up to "junk food," for example, when it was more likely to have resulted from toxic thoughts and habits of thinking that took their toll on your overall health. As noted by Caroline Leaf,

> *No system of the body is spared when stress is running rampant. A massive body of research collectively shows that up to 80% of physical, emotional, and mental health issues today could be a direct result of our thought lives... Thoughts are not only scientifically measurable, but we can verify how they affect our bodies. We can actually feel our thoughts through our emotions. Emotions are involved in every thought we build, ever built and ever will build.*[31]

We live in a fast-paced world full of stressful circumstances and emotions. Each day, we have the choice to take charge of our thoughts and control how stress affects us. We can break the cycle of toxic thinking and toxic habits. Being aware of how toxic thought affects various organs and systems along the way is very important.

Your most vital muscle organ, the heart, is more than just a pump to sustain life. Your heart is sensitive to what you think and feel; in other words, your thoughts directly affect your heart.

Here are some examples of various heart conditions in which stress is a major contributor:

- *Hypertension—high blood pressure*
- *Angina—chest pain and spasms of the heart tissue*
- *Coronary artery disease—hardening of the arteries causing a narrowing, which can be triggered by anger*
- *Strokes or cerebrovascular insufficiency—clogging of blood vessels so that brain tissue becomes starved*
- *Aneurysm—ballooning or swelling of a blood vessel on the artery or rupturing of blood vessels.*[32]

The reality is that your heart is in constant communication with your brain and the rest of your body. The signals your heart sends to your brain influence not just perception and emotional and processing functions, but higher cognitive functions as well. Current research on the heart's neurological sensitivity indicates that there are lines of communication between the brain and the heart that check the accuracy and integrity of your thought life.

In addition, your immune system and digestive system are highly sensitive to your thought life and habits. When your immune system faces an attack of toxic thinking, it weakens the immune system by preventing it from doing what it was naturally designed to do. Your habits and the way you process stress in dealing with toxic thoughts and emotions can lower immunity; however, the effects of the day-to-day stress over time can confuse the autoimmune system response and cause your body to turn on itself, attacking healthy cells and tissues. Have you ever noticed that you get sick when you take a vacation or an extended period of rest? This is a perfect example of how the daily stresses of life add up to negatively affect thinking and habits of life and progressively weaken the immune system.

There is evidence showing that your digestive system comes under attack from toxic thinking and habits as well. Your digestive system works hard under normal conditions to get as many nutrients as possible from everything you eat and drink to keep your bodily processes and organs in an optimal state. However, we know that thinking and emotions have an impact on the levels of stress chemicals released, which invade the digestive system and create a poisonous cocktail that damages your health.

Some digestive disorders that can originate from the effects of toxic thoughts and emotions include the following:

- *Constipation*
- *Diarrhea*
- *Nausea and vomiting*
- *Cramping*
- *Ulcers*
- *Leaking-gut syndrome—when nutrients leak out of your stomach and colon walls and don't make it to your cells*
- *Irritable bowel syndrome (spastic colon)—when the intestines either squeeze too hard or not hard enough, reducing optimum absorption of nutrients*[33]

This is the bad news, but there is good news as well. Ancient, timeless principles and neuroscience clearly demonstrate the link between your thoughts, emotions, and habits and your physical, mental, and spiritual well-being. The more you manage your thought life and habits, the more you will be able to listen to them and deal constructively with them. Making your habits and inner thought life a priority is a life-giving action rather than a life-threatening one, and it will improve your overall wellness and decrease your vulnerability to sickness and disease.

Neuroscience calls this process *self-directed neuroplasticity*; you may be familiar with the spiritual aspect of the process called the "renewing of your mind" (Romans 12:2). **You are not a slave of your habits or chained**

to your thoughts. You can choose to be free from toxic thoughts and memories that have hindered your personal greatness. In the chapters that follow, we will dive deeper into how you can transform your thinking and habits of heart to affect your leadership influence and legacy significantly, both personally and professionally.

CHAPTER 16

THE HEAD OF A SERVANT LEADER: HABIT MODEL— ATTENTION: KEY TO CHANGE

> *Attention is a mental muscle; like any other muscle, it can be strengthened through the right kind of exercise.*
> —DANIEL GOLEMAN

Do you have trouble remembering what someone has just told you in conversation? Did you drive to work this morning on autopilot? Do you focus more on your smartphone than on the person you're having lunch with?

The fundamental exercise for building deliberate attention is simple: **When your mind wanders, notice that it has wandered, bring it back to your desired point of focus, and keep it there as long as you can.** That basic exercise is at the root of virtually every kind of meditation and reflective practice. Meditation and reflection build concentration and calmness and facilitate recovery from the agitation of stress. *Attention is a mental muscle, and like all other muscles, it must be exercised.*

Attention
Understanding the power of attention is the key to transformational change.
We to take A.I.M. (Attention focus, inhibit negative, Memory built on the positive) on our thinking moment by moment day by day.

Attention is the basis of the most essential servant leadership skills— **the human quality of connecting and empathizing with and relating to others**. The world we live in is constantly attacking our ability to focus our attention. This essential servant leadership skill has been under greater assault as we progress through the twenty-first century. If servant leaders are to direct the attention of others toward collaboration, strategy, and innovation, they must first learn to focus their own attention in *three ways: first on themselves, second on others, and then on the wider world.*

Every servant leader needs to cultivate these three areas of awareness, both in abundance and in the proper balance, because a failure to focus inward leaves one rudderless, a failure to focus on others renders one clueless, and a failure to focus outward may cause one to be blindsided. The good news is that practically every form of focus can be strengthened.

Daniel Goleman, the author of *Emotional Intelligence, Social Intelligence, Focus*, and many other books on the power of cultivating awareness, explains why focus is crucial to great leadership:

Focused leaders can command the full range of their own attention: They are in touch with their inner feelings, they can control their impulses, they are aware of how others see them, and they can weed out distractions and also allow their minds to roam widely, free of preconceptions.[34]

The primary task of servant leadership is to direct attention. **To do so, leaders must learn to focus their own attention.** When we speak about being focused, we commonly mean thinking about one thing while filtering out distractions. But a wealth of recent research in neuroscience shows that we focus in many ways, for different purposes, drawing on different neural pathways—some of which work in concert, whereas others tend to stand in opposition.

Neuroscience and ancient wisdom tell us that attention is the key to unlocking transformational change and personal greatness. When we pay attention to something repeatedly, the necessary wiring in the brain is formed that makes it possible for us to learn new things, take the right actions, and achieve our goals. Research shows that driving that attention through repetition is critical to establishing neural and new connections and therefore new learning, growth, and insights. **Neurons that fire together wire together** is a simple but profound axiom that underscores this fundamental truth.

Although attention is essential, it is not enough. We need to inhibit distraction and/or negative thoughts and build positive memory. In *Boundaries for Leaders*, Dr. Henry Cloud developed a framework around the brain's executive function:

Whether driving a car or making or selling cars, the brain relies on three essential processes:

> **Attention:** *the ability to focus on relevant stimuli, and block out what is not relevant: "Pay attention!"* **Inhibition:** *the ability to "not do" certain actions that could be distracting, irrelevant, or even destructive: "Don't do that!"* **Working Memory:** *the ability to retain and access relevant information for reasoning, decision-making, and taking future actions: "Remember and build on relevant information." In other words, our brains need to be able to (a) focus on something specific, (b) not get off track by focusing on or being assaulted by other data inputs or toxicity, and (c) continuously be aware of relevant information at all times.*[35]

Using Dr. Cloud's framework, I put together a working model to take **AIM on habits** and transform thinking. The model has been used in the *Servant Leadership Coaching System* training process.

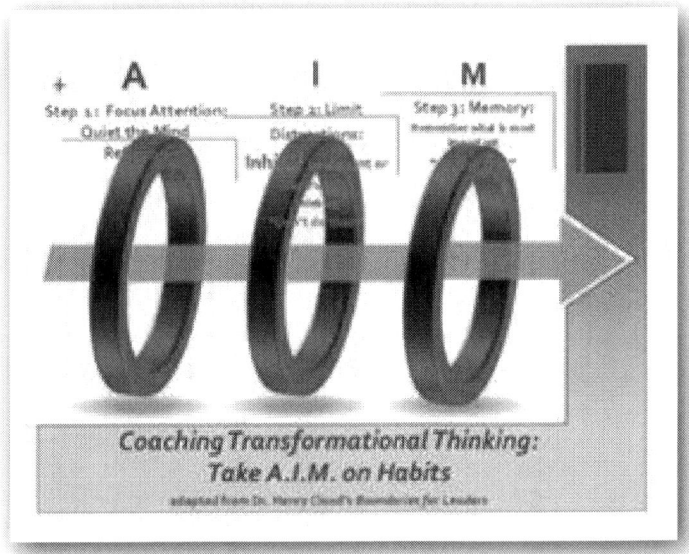

We live in very fast-paced, stressful, and many times toxic environments, all of which adds to the lack of attention or a form of attention deficit disorder or wandering-mind syndrome. Clarity comes before action, and we can't take action if we are confused, fragmented, anxious, and stressed. **It calls for us to be able to take control of the day by taking charge of the moment.** Every thought does matter. You can take **AIM** on your habits of thinking and experience a transformed mind and life. We all crave focused attention, positivity, unity, control, and a sense of truly serving others productively. It all begins with strengthening the muscle of attention.

In my personal experience, research, and coaching practice, I have seen the power of attention strengthened and developed by following a simple plan. The plan is simple; it is the practice that is difficult. However, those who have taken the challenge—including me—have been transformed over a period of thirty to sixty days.

The Sixty-Day Challenge for Building Focus of Attention

1. **Make a purposeful shift in your thinking and calendar to focus on relationships over task.** Our modern world has put us on the treadmill of busyness and task focus. The harassed and helpless mind-set I described in the opening chapters has made us very task or "I"-focused in all of our interactions. We have become all about just getting things done versus how can we really serve the needs of others. This shift is simple, but it will have a profound effect on how you approach your daily schedule, both at home and at work.

   After hearing about the sixty-day challenge to build the muscle of focus of attention, a busy central office school administrator took action by changing the background wallpaper of her smartphone. She simply printed in the background *Relationship over task.* She reported that even after one week, let alone thirty to sixty days, this simple reminder was having an amazing effect on all of her interactions:

   > *I thought I was connected and very relational until I realized how "task" focused I had become. What I have come to realize is that my focus really wasn't on people; it was simply getting to the next task, next meeting, and, honestly, just getting my family to the right event or activity. When I refocused every interaction and conversation with a simple reminder of who am I talking to, what is most important to them, and how can I connect with them, I found that my family, my coworkers, and my direct reports responded and were much more open. However, as I have been building this habit over the past sixty days, I can see what is happening inside of me. I am changing and really being present in the moment for what is most important, people!*[86]

2. **Schedule a "five-minute" reboot before every interaction.** Although the key to rewiring your brain and ultimately your habits

of mind is to focus on *relationship over task*, you need to literally "reboot" the brain before every interaction. Just as a computer with applications open over a period of time begins to run slower and is not as functional, we humans need to be aware that our focus of attention has limits; it loses strength over time, and we become sluggish in our thinking. Thus, like a computer, we need a reboot to refresh, reframe, and refocus our attention. Before every interaction, take **a five-minute reboot time** to recharge your focus on *relationship before task*. The reboot time accomplishes three things. **First, it allows you time to breathe and calm your mind; second, it allows you to think about whom you are talking or interacting with; and third, it gives you time in your schedule to reflect.**

a. **Breathing:** The *reticular activating system* (RAS) is the portal through which nearly all information enters the brain. The RAS filters the incoming information and affects what you pay attention to, how aroused you are, and what is not going to get access to all of your brain. It is the key that turns the brain on or off, more or less, although it would be better to say it is the key that turns the brain and the body up or down.

   Focused deep breathing activates and/or controls the RAS because the *breath* and the *body* are interconnected. We are always breathing to sustain life, but we are not always conscious of our breathing. The entire exercise only takes **six seconds**! Take a deep breath in and hold it, then let it out slowly for six seconds. Repeat the process four to six times, and you will start to feel calm and relaxed and have a better ability to focus.

b. **Relational interaction:** Now that you are relaxed and more focused, ask yourself these three questions: (1) *With whom am I going to interact?* (2) *Right now, what is most important to this person?* (3) *How am I going to approach this interaction or conversation?*

c. **Reflection:** During the five-minute reboot, be reflective by being in tune with your inner attitude and then allowing yourself to be other-centered. Enhance your leadership impact and influence by making human connections habitually, intentionally, and purposefully.

After being exposed to the sixty-day challenge to build the muscle of attention, a busy senior-level business executive reported to a servant leadership training team on the power of the five-minute reboot:

> *I can't tell you how much my life has been changed over the past sixty days. It has been an amazing experience in both my personal and professional lives. First, I took the suggestion to do the five-minute reboot before every interaction and meeting and to just stop and do the deep breathing. My sense of anxiousness has been lowered, and my ability to concentrate on what is most important in the moment has been enhanced.*
>
> *At work, I am scheduling my meetings differently. I no longer schedule the meetings that I am in charge of on the hour; instead, I start meetings ten minutes past the hour (e.g., 9:10 a.m.) and run thirty- to fifty-minute meetings. If meetings run longer, I try to cut them off no later than five minutes after the hour. This gives me time to reboot for the next meeting and be focused on whom I am meeting with and what is most important. The results have been amazing. Not only do I feel more connected and in tune, but others have noticed that the quality of our meetings is more "we" focused and productive.*
>
> *On my ride home, I reboot and think about my wife and what is most important for her in that moment. I have thought about specific questions that progressively build connection with her. With my two children, I am more in the moment with them, and we have purposely focused on how to connect with each one of them individually. I can only tell you in tears that this has been transformational for me and my family.*[37]

Recently, a woman expressed how the five-minute reboot process has been instrumental in relieving her anxiety and high blood pressure:

> *I thought I was going to have a heart attack! I had severe pains in my chest and felt like someone was sitting on my chest. After a series of tests*

with a cardiologist, he concluded that it was not a heart issue but a result of stress. My stress levels had caused me to have high blood pressure and panic attacks. Through the process of gaining control of the anxiety and stress, I realized my thinking and mind-set were causing this problem. Over time, I was obsessing about things I couldn't control and developed a very negative focus that was not only impacting me but all of my relationships and interactions. The simple process of the five-minute reboot that begins with deep breathing and refocusing your mind has lowered my blood pressure and given me a sense of calm in the middle of life's storms. Over the course of the sixty days, I noticed a significant decrease in this heaviness in my chest and felt more relaxed and at peace than I had in quite a while. Recently, during a checkup with my cardiologist, I was taken off my blood pressure medication. When I sense the anxiety or rising stress levels, I immediately start the reboot process.[38]

The five-minute reboot, as you can see from the previous testimonies, can be transformational and begin the process of renewing your mind-set. Building the muscle of attention is not just a skill for a servant leader; it is a process that can change every life.

Question for Reflection

1. Do you suffer from a wandering mind and the inability to focus?
2. Are your interactions—professional and personal—connected, empathetic, and relational?
3. Are your current habits of mind enhancing your life or impeding it?
4. Do you have an accountability partner or group to help you in this process?

Steps for Action

1. Take the Sixty-Day Challenge and follow the steps outlined in this chapter.

2. After thirty days, note any changes in your ability to focus, hear, and listen.
3. What kind of feedback are you getting from others as a result of the Sixty-Day Challenge?

CHAPTER 17

THE HEAD OF A SERVANT LEADER: HABIT MODEL APPROACH— BUILD CONNECTION: EMPATHY

Seek first to understand, then to be understood.
—STEPHEN R. COVEY

A great deal of conflict that we experience with people could be reduced or eliminated if we simply tried to understand other people's points of view before we tried to convince them of our own message. We need to listen with the intention of understanding what others are trying to say. ***Empathy is the ability to understand and relate to the emotions of others.*** It helps us to walk in the shoes of another person or to see things from another's point of view. The ability to master the power of connection to enhance our relationships with others is essential, and in exercising this ability, we all become smarter at navigating our social highways. **Servant leadership is not about how smart we are; it is about how open we are to learning new and effective ways to connect and build trust, partnership, and mutual success.**

Empathy is one of the most important parts of social awareness and perhaps one of the most critical people skills for servant leaders. *Social awareness* is the ability to understand the emotions of others. It includes the competencies of empathy, group awareness, seeing others clearly, and emotional boundaries. Simply put, social awareness is the ability to read situations and people accurately and to understand and empathize with the emotions of others.

Build

As humans, we need connection and we build connection though empathy.

Our ability to see, hear, and feel with others. People don't care how much you know until they know how much you care.

Too many interactions miss the mark. We talk past and over one another, and we make up things that suit our motivations and needs. We don't notice the little cues that people are sending our way that would, if properly reacted to, enhance connection and trust. We are distracted, and as a result, we are not in the moment and aware of the human beings all around us. Our busy, "wandering" mind-sets have affected our ability to connect and ultimately understand and empathize with others. We can connect 24/7 from anywhere in the world at any time, but it's not enough to have the tools to connect. ***We need to have the wisdom to connect.***

Many neuroscientists have compared the importance of the landmark discovery of mirror neurons in the 1990s as ranking alongside the discovery of DNA. Mirror neurons give humans the **ability to learn through imitation**—you watch someone do something, and you imitate it. The more you copy someone's action, the easier it becomes; eventually, you can do it almost without thinking.

Research indicates that the basic need for relatedness, empathy, and bonding is actually a biological wiring that is activated through such a learning process. Bonding can be learned by watching others and experiencing how they bond. The mirror-neuron system provides scientific validation of the need for empathy and authenticity in order to engage and inspire others.

Connecting with others also involves picking up on the "signals" they are sending about themselves, their emotions, and their needs. Signals are the verbal and nonverbal messages that confirm or deny the truth of a person's communications. Most signals are subtle. Sometimes signals are conscious, whereas others operate at the subconscious level.

Four main sources of human signals are part of the verbal or nonverbal exchanges between people:

- **Body:** *Body language* includes gestures, posture, facial expressions, and tone of voice. These can be conscious or unconscious, positive or negative.
- **Emotions:** Examples of basic emotions are anger, fear, joy, sadness, disgust, and surprise. These emotions activate the body, which in turn sends out signals.
- **Mind:** You send signals about what is going on in your mind. What you think becomes a signal, often (but not always) through the words that you use. What you believe about the other person affects the signals you send.
- **Spirit:** Spirit indicates the intention that is behind all other signals: your purpose, your motivation while you are taking action, and your end goal. Signals from the spirit convey a sense of judgment.

Over the past five years, I have been investigating both formally and informally the correlation between the role of the leader and the leader's empathy levels. **I have concluded that as a person's leadership role in an organization increases, his or her empathy levels and self-awareness decrease.** There is a multitude of variables that can affect this correlation, but one primary factor that strikes me is what we have discussed throughout this book as the ***harassed and helpless mind-set*** that leads to a weakening of our focus of attention on others. As a leadership role increases, a person can become more **task**-focused; as a result, the muscle of attention on others atrophies. Thus, we become **less self-aware and, ultimately, less "other" aware.**

In our *Servant Leadership Coaching System* training, we assess the emotional intelligence of leaders through an online assessment called the **EIQ-16** (MySkillsprofile.com). This assessment has been given to approximately one hundred leaders, from both the business and educational leadership sectors, in our initial testing process. Our research has found that both middle-level and senior-level leaders—regardless of sector—scored below the norms established by the EIQ-16 in two areas: **being in touch with their own emotions, and reading others and relating to them**. In other words, these leaders scored slightly lower than the average in their ability to read themselves accurately and relate to others. This sample size is not very large, and further formal research needs to be done; however, many other experts, including Daniel Goleman, author of *Focus: The Hidden Driver of Excellence*, are suggesting the same type of correlation. Goleman notes:

> *There is an intriguing relationship between self-awareness and power. There are relatively few gaps between one's ratings among lower-level employees.* ***But the higher someone's position in an organization, the bigger the gap.*** *Self-awareness seems to diminish with promotions up the organizational ladder...A lack of self-awareness leaves you clueless.*
>
> *One theory: That the gap widens because as people rise in power within the organization the circle shrinks of others willing or courageous enough to speak to them honestly about their quirks. Then there are those who simply deny their deficits, or can't see them in the first place.*[39]

Mirror neurons have particular importance in organizations because leaders' emotions and actions prompt followers to mirror those feelings and deeds. The effects of activating neural circuitry in followers' brains can be very powerful. A recent study observed two groups: one received negative performance feedback accompanied by positive emotional signals—namely nods and smiles; the other was given positive feedback that was delivered critically, with frowns and narrowed eyes. In subsequent interviews conducted to compare the emotional states of the two groups, the people who had received positive feedback accompanied by negative emotional signals reported feeling worse about their performance than did the participants who had received good-natured negative feedback. **In effect, the delivery was more important than the message itself.** And everybody knows that when people feel better, they perform better. So, if leaders hope to get the best out of others, they should continue to be demanding, but in ways that foster a positive mood in their teams. The old carrot-and-stick approach alone doesn't make neural sense; traditional incentive systems are simply not enough to get the best performance from followers.

Here's an example of what does work. It turns out that there's a subset of mirror neurons whose only job is to detect other people's smiles and laughter, prompting smiles and laughter in return. A leader who is self-controlled and humorless will rarely engage those neurons in team members, but a leader who laughs and sets an easygoing tone puts those neurons to work, triggering spontaneous laughter and knitting his or her team together in the process.

We can pass on good or bad feelings and "infect" the well-being of others. Our moods and emotions, both positive and negative, are contagious. We need to ask ourselves the following kinds of questions: *What kind of mood and energy am I fostering when I enter a room? When I give feedback? When I make a request? When I make a correction? When I communicate one-on-one or in a group? How do people perceive me? What kind of climate and culture am I creating and allowing?*

How do servant leaders increase empathy? It begins with becoming more self-aware and understanding and taking control of your own emotional state, attitude, and mood. A servant leader who is in touch with his or her internal state and in the moment recognizes triggers that lead to bad or negative emotions and will increasingly see his or her empathy levels increase over time.

Two simple internal checks can help increase your empathy. **First, be aware of how you are reacting to a person, situation, or circumstance.** Is there a pattern that triggers a negative or bad emotional reaction? Certain people or situations can trigger internal feelings, such as anger, disgust, rage, or fear, distrust, stress, and so forth. Simply identifying the emotion and putting it into words, according to neuroscientists, reduces the level of stress or anxiety. In addition, by labeling the emotion internally, we are able to begin the process of self-awareness. If we lack the capacity to monitor our emotions, we will be poorly suited to manage or learn from them. If we are not tuned in to our experience, we will find it all the more difficult to be attuned to the emotions of others.

A senior manager of a company had a habit of sending out e-mails that were frequently filled with words that gave the recipients the feeling that the manager had **"caught them"** doing something wrong or that revealed recipients' mistakes. The e-mails were pointed and accusatory in tone. Whenever this manager saw something requiring attention, she reacted and sent out an e-mail. Over time, the well-meaning manager had created a fear-based work culture because of her way of communicating. What she didn't realize was that she did it out of fear—fear of losing control, fear of failure, and fear that those under her supervision were lazy or not as productive as they could be. She was not self-aware; as a result, she projected her own fears onto others.

Are you a thermometer or thermostat? A thermometer simply reacts to the temperature of the environment. However, a thermostat is different. It regulates the climate and environment and controls the temperature. By simply becoming more self-aware and identifying how you are feeling by putting the feeling to words, you begin the process of building connection and empathy because you are more in tune with your internal state of mind.

The second internal check is to think before you react. Ask yourself: *How would others feel or take what I am going to say or do?* If the senior manager in the previous example would have used this technique before hitting the Send button, she would have saved herself the bigger issue of the toxic, fear-based culture she was creating around her. She could have avoided the unintended outcome by rereading her e-mails and asking *How are the recipients going to receive this? If I were in their shoes, how would I* *receive this message?* **Remember, communication is never what we think we communicated; it is what the receiver actually hears.**

You might think that the impact of such a simple approach would be minor; however, in my experience, these two internal checks can and do produce transformational change in the ability to empathize with others.

Listening That Connects: The 70/30 Principle

Servant leaders are most effective when they listen and ask questions. *Talk less, listen more, and ask more questions than you give answers—that is key to those who lead by serving.* I recommend the **70/30 principle** discussed earlier. When we listen to others and then ask appropriate questions *70 percent of the time*, we facilitate understanding, connection, understanding of different perspectives, and, ultimately, powerful collaborative relationships.

Listening is a very complex process. Think about your last really great conversation. *What made it great? Was it the speaking or the listening or some combination of both?* Typically, we do not give much thought to listening, and if we do, the main concern is whether or not we were listened *to*. The reality is that how we listen shapes and influences how we connect to others.

Listening that connects is not about waiting for others to stop talking. It is about being engaged with another person or persons in such a way that the focus is on understanding not only their words, but also the meaning of those words. It is a discovery process, and the focus cannot be on what you are thinking, or your preconceived conceptions that filter your hearing, or about your view or your opinion. It's about quieting your internal dialogue and being fully in tune and present—generating acceptance, safety, and appreciation while others speak—and it's about allowing another person or persons to truly be heard.

THE HEART, HEAD, AND HANDS OF A SERVANT LEADER

When we ask questions that help others reflect on their own thinking, help them discover or affirm what or how they feel, or help them to clarify a problem or issue, we are creating a safe place and fostering more collaborative relationships. The following can help to facilitate reflection in others:

It sounds like you have been thinking about this for quite a long time.

Tell me more about what you are thinking.

What is most important to you right now?

If you follow your current line of thinking, what is the best thing that can happen? What is the worst?

It sounds like you are struggling with this. Tell me more about when you first became aware of the struggle.

How are you feeling right now about what you just said?

Whom do you talk to when you have these feelings?

When you do speak, instead of giving opinions or advice, use what you have discovered about things you have in common and share a story from your personal experience. People relate to stories and personal experience. In your story, be vulnerable by relating your own struggle, and show your appreciation of the other person's point of view. Keep in mind that this conversation is not about you; it is about the other person or persons. Therefore, keep the balance of the 70/30 principle in the forefront of your mind.

People really don't care how much you know until they feel and experience how much you really care. Listening that connects allows you the opportunity to become a trusted adviser and a person who leads by serving the needs of others.

A senior-level leader in one of our servant leader training groups reported on the power of the 70/30 principle both personal and professionally:

My wife has told me that I have "husband ears"—I only act like I am listening to her. Over the years, this has been a joke she tells others; however, it wasn't until the training session on the power of connection and empathy that I realized that this was not only true but painfully negatively impacting our family. To be honest, as I reflected on my listening skills and my lack of empathy, I literally wept. It hit me like a ton of bricks. My wife and family deserve better, and I wanted to make a significant change.

I wanted to focus my attention on building relationships through connected listening, so I have been building and practicing the skill of the 70/30 principle over the past sixty days. In tears, I have to tell you that my relationship with my wife and kids has dramatically changed. I feel like I am present and in the moment because I am hearing and asking questions that connect with them. My wife told me the other day that she feels so loved by me because she feels like I really am hearing and getting her. My college-age son said to me that he didn't feel like I was trying to control him anymore, but allowing him to make his own decisions. Wow, how simple just to listen and ask questions.

Professionally, this practice of the 70/30 principle has helped me not to be such a micromanager of my direct reports. I ask questions to which I don't have the answers and make them think about their own thinking. One of my direct reports told me that for the first time in her life, someone really believes in her. When I probed what she meant by that, she said, "You don't talk at me; you listen and talk with me." I know I still have a long way to go, but as you say, "Progression not perfection."[10]

Questions for Reflection

1. Do you sense that your empathy levels need to be refocused and reframed?
2. How in touch are you with your own feelings?

3. If others were to be honest with you, would they say that they feel connected and cared about in your daily interactions with them?
4. What steps or skills from this chapter are you going to apply in your personal and professional lives?

Steps for Action

1. Take an assessment of your current level of empathy (e.g. EIQ16).
2. What do the results tell you, and on what area or areas do you need to focus?
3. Practice listening to connect through the 70/30 principle for the next thirty days.

CHAPTER 18

The Head of a Servant Leader: HABIT Model— Inhibit: Negative Thinking Patterns

> *In the end, as a leader, you are always going to get a combination of two things; what you create and what you allow.*
> —Dr. Henry Cloud

GIGO is a term in computer software that means **garbage in = garbage out.** Likewise, what we create and allow in our minds will affect how we live. Allowing negative thinking patterns is like putting toxic waste into our systems, which will affect our overall well-being. What we put into our minds and our thinking will come out in our attitudes, actions, and behaviors. **We become what we think.** Negative thinking corrodes our operating systems, causing a sluggish and corrupted programming of our strength of mind. However, our thinking patterns can be mastered and controlled; we don't have to be hindered or stuck.

You are not doomed to repeat the patterns of thinking that you have acquired over time or that have been repeated in your family. You are not controlled by your biology, and you can transcend the influence of your environment. If you have been told something different, you have been misled and lied to.

The truth is, no matter how toxic your thinking, background, biology, memories, or environment, there is hope. You can break the chains that have been limiting your development into your unique, God-given "sweet spot" of greatness. Ancient wisdom and modern science affirm that we can reframe, reshape, and transform our heart mind-sets.

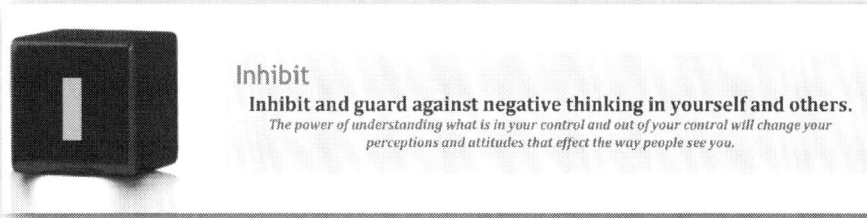

Inhibit
Inhibit and guard against negative thinking in yourself and others.
The power of understanding what is in your control and out of your control will change your perceptions and attitudes that effect the way people see you.

That's why I get excited to share with you what I have found and what many others are now experiencing. I want to make principles and research simple so that everyone can understand and can learn enough to have the clarity to take action to overcome negative thinking patterns and experience the joy, freedom, and confidence of living in the "sweet spot" of greatness.

Be a "Gatekeeper" of Your Thinking

The definition of a gatekeeper is as follows: *an attendant at a gate who is employed to control who goes through it; a person or thing that controls access to something.* One of the reasons we get stuck in negative thinking patterns is because we create and allow negative thinking to overwhelm our thoughts, and as a result, we become less and less aware of spotting it and denying it access to our brains and, ultimately, our heart mind-set. You must become a gatekeeper and take control of what gets access to your heart mind-set because every thought does matter.

Your prevailing thinking patterns will define your attitudes, values, and, ultimately, your character. **Are you spotting and addressing negative and toxic thinking patterns?** We have established that *servant leadership is more caught than taught*; it comes from modeling and example first and foremost. We know that as we think in our hearts about ourselves, we become who we are meant to be. We also know that what proceeds out of our mouth reflects what is in our hearts. Therefore, we must become intentional gatekeepers of our thinking, spotting negative and toxic thoughts and then controlling them and taking them captive.

Dr. Henry Cloud, in his book *Boundaries for Leaders*, identified two major categories of negative thinking patterns.[41] Through my reading, research, and development of training programs for servant leaders, I have incorporated these two categories into the training process.

1. "It Can't Be Done" Virus

This form of negative thinking pattern is like a computer virus slowing down or shutting down our personal operating systems. ***When the general pattern of thinking focuses on problems, blame, disappointments, dependency, reactivity, finger-pointing, not taking responsibility, ignoring, or even denying, we become negative thinkers.*** This is what happens when people and organizations find themselves thinking and behaving in a manner that the authors of *The Oz Principle* call *below the line*.[42] Operating below the line happens whenever we consciously or unconsciously avoid accountability for individual or collective results and get stuck in what the authors call the *victim cycle* or *blame game*. In this cycle, you begin to lose your spirit and resolve until, eventually, you feel completely powerless; you are stuck in "I can't!"

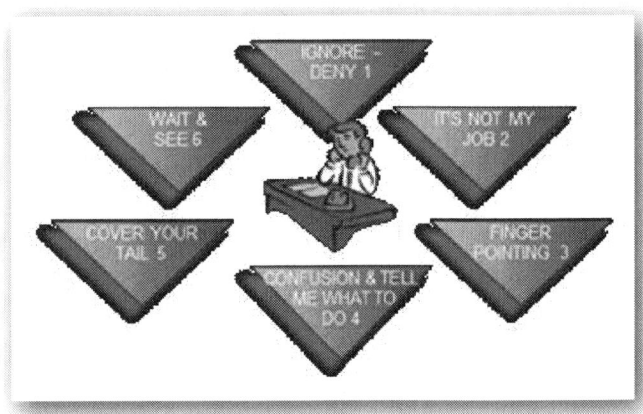

Below-the-line thinking refers to a particular mind-set that shapes how you view the world in a limiting way. It leads to the belief that what's happening to you is outside of your control and is everyone else's fault—the economy, your industry, your boss, your spouse, and so forth. Below-the-line thinking says, *It's not fair what's happening, and I don't have what it takes to overcome these challenges. I didn't expect this, and I can't handle it.*

2. Learned Helplessness Default Thinking

Learned helplessness default thinking is a change in the brain's "software" that takes place when it is confronted with the continued negativity that you feel you have absolutely no control over. In other words, the brain tells your entire system to go passive and shut down. We were designed to have a certain amount of control over our well-being. We are born with the innate desire to own and control what happens to us. However, through negative patterns and experiences over time, we can start to develop a state of mind that gets reinforced, resulting in the development of a default thinking pattern in which we believe that we have absolutely no control over what happens to us. The perceived lack of control over things affects our overall well-being.

Dr. Henry Cloud describes how patterns of thinking involving powerlessness and helplessness first came to light when experimenters subjected dogs to a small electrical shock:

> *In the first part of the experiment, the dogs received a shock but could do nothing to avoid the shock. The dogs were then exposed to another small electrical shock that they could easily escape. Nevertheless, the dogs responded passively and gave up trying, even in the face of this new option. The first part of the experiment had taught them that they were helpless to act and to avoid suffering, and even when there was something they could do when they were given some control again, they had learned to accept their helplessness and do nothing. Put another way, their software had been reprogrammed: from "feel the pain and do something" to "if you feel pain, there is nothing you can do, so do nothing."*[13]

This is an example of the same passivity that people often learn as they grow up in homes where they feel powerless. Negativity and toxicity are realities; learned helplessness default thinking is a choice. In learned helplessness, our brains and minds consciously and unconsciously shift and go into passive or shut-down mode; imitative behavior, creativity, and problem-solving stop. It is simply "game over." We are paralyzed in our heart mind-set and are operating out of fear.

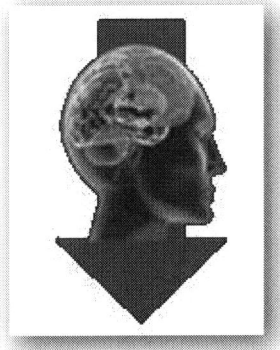

When fear is triggered in the brain, the result is a fight, flight, fright, or freeze response. We are operating out of the lower part of the brain, which goes into survival mode. *Amygdala hijack* is the term used by neuroscientists to describe what happens when fear is triggered and we are operating out of stress. When the amygdala goes into overdrive, it activates the limbic area of the brain, which stores all of our old memories. Once triggered, this part of the brain begins to remember other similar hurts and threats, and it lumps them all together. Without our even realizing it, our minds can take old memories and edit them into a familiar movie, giving our current situation the same feel that flips on the default mode of learned helplessness.

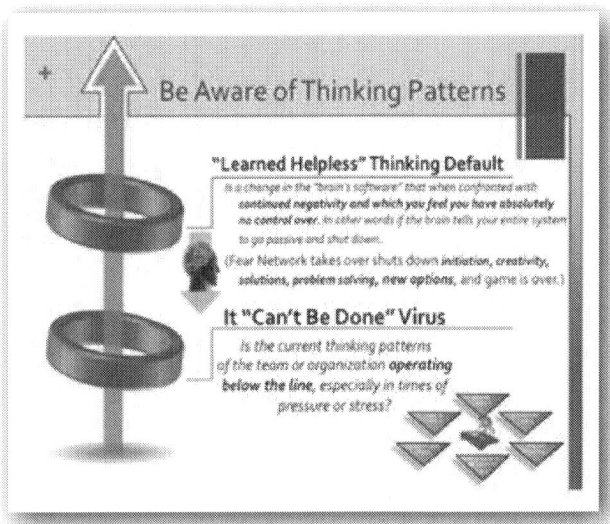

Negative thinking patterns are not just some psychological jargon; they affect the way we think and live. We know that it is possible to reverse the effects of the "it can't be done" virus and learned helplessness default thinking. Even if you are consumed by toxic thinking because of one or both of these patterns or live in a toxic environment that is discouraging, you can take control of your thought life. You can break the chains that have been limiting your development into you unique personal "sweet spot" of greatness. The brain is truly incredible; it can be reshaped and reformed:

> *Detoxifying your thoughts can be like selecting a book from a shelf in your library of memories, rewriting a page in that book, then placing it back on the shelf, free of toxic thoughts and emotions. If it happens to be a life-threatening book, you may want to do even more work on it and even get rid of the book altogether. That is part of the process of building a new healthy thought… The good news is we can change those pathways within four days and create new ones in twenty-one days.*[44]

Martin Seligman's groundbreaking research on thinking style, as presented in *Boundaries for Leaders* by Henry Cloud, led to the creation of three categories of thinking patterns that he calls the 3Ps:[45]

The 3Ps of Negative Thinking Patterns

1. **Personalizing**: When you explain an event, circumstance, or situation in relationship to yourself in a negative direction—for example: *I'm such a lousy husband/wife. I am a loser. I am not convincing when I talk to customers. I have no credibility. No one wants what I have to offer. I'm just not very good.*
   In other words, you think the event occurred because you are *not good enough.*
2. **Pervasive:** Instead of seeing a situation as a specific, isolated event, applying to just this one thing, you generalize it to make it be about everything. It goes from a single event to a pervasive reality—for example: *It isn't just my spouse; everyone thinks this*

about me. *All of my coworkers feel the same way about me. I can't catch a break because everybody thinks this about me. Every time I turn around, everything is ready to fall apart. The whole world is against me.* A single event triggers such thoughts and is interpreted in a negative way that pervades and dominates the whole picture. Everything begins to look negative.

In other words, in your mind, *nothing is going well or will go well for you.*

3. **Permanent:** Instead of seeing this event as a single event or a single point in time, you see it as permanent. Your thinking is stuck in the belief that this is just the way it is, and nothing will ever change for you—for example: *Why even try; nothing is going to change. The good old days are gone forever. We will never make it; it is impossible. I wish I could make changes, but every time I try, it never works for me.* This thinking says the current negative event is not something that will eventually pass but has become "the way it is, and the way it will be forever." It is your new normal. In short, there is just no hope and no reason to hope. **In other words, you think** *nothing is going to be any different, so why try?*

Reversing the 3Ps of Negative Thinking Patterns

Using Dr. Henry Cloud's advice of auditing your own thinking, I have personally experienced the transformational results of reframing and reshaping my thinking. In addition, working with our servant leadership training teams, we have seen others take charge and transform negative thinking patterns.

Observe, Log, Refute

We have incorporated a process of monitoring 3P negative thinking patterns through observing, logging, and refuting over the course of sixty days. Participants were given a small spiral notebook and asked to log consciously over a sixty-day training cycle their thinking each time they noticed negative patterns in relation to the 3Ps. **They logged and labeled each thought and then gave an argument to counter the negative thought.**

By grasping the negative thought through writing it down, identifying what it is, and then providing the counterargument, you start the internal process of reversing negative thinking one thought at a time. Let's consider a few negative thoughts and their counterarguments:

- When overwhelmed with a new opportunity, the magnitude of the project starts to trigger this thought: *I'm not good enough to pull this off. I'm going to fail miserably.* Notice that this is personalizing and focusing on your inadequacies and fears. The counterargument could be, *I just have to take one step at a time and control what I can control. I can execute and do the very best I can right now.*
- *Everything is going south; nothing we are doing is working.* This is an example of pervasive thinking. You overgeneralize, and in your thoughts, you see this event or situation as controlling everything. The counter argument could be, *Not everything is bad; I need to look at the big picture. This is related to this one situation, not everything.*
- *It is not going to be different tomorrow; this always happens to me. Nothing ever changes.* This is an example of permanent thinking; you are caught in your thoughts of believing that you are stuck in this pattern forever. Many people believe they are victims and cannot escape from their thoughts, which now have become their reality. The counterargument could be, *Keep moving. Each day I can change this; everything changes over time, and I too can change. I am not a victim, and I can control my thoughts and focus on a better reality.*

Negative thinking patterns can also be a combination of all of the 3Ps and may be hard to sort out. However, if you can name it, you can tame it. The power of positive self-talk can renew your thinking, create new wiring in your brain, and reverse the effects of **negativity**, the **"I can't" virus**, and **learned helplessness**.

An educator who had been suffering from stress reported to me after going through this process over the course of sixty days that she felt like she was taking charge of her thought life and was experiencing an internal peace through this simple exercise. She commented:

My situation or circumstances have not changed, but I am taking control of my reactions. This exercise has been life changing. Not only am I lowering my stress levels, but for the first time in many years I am experiencing restful sleep and feel energized.[46]

A middle-level manager who had been struggling with depression and a sense of hopelessness stated:

I know people have recognized my mood and attitude at home and work, but I didn't realize how depressed I have become. My thoughts were overwhelming me, and I felt like I had no control, a victim. There were times when I just felt like this was my life, and nothing was ever going to change. I am so thankful for this exercise; it is changing my life one thought at a time. I have to admit, it is hard, but now I feel like I can take control of my thoughts, and I have hope. I have tools and weapons to combat my own negative thoughts.[47]

Another participant reported that she struggled with self-confidence and self-image:

After sixty days, I realized that what I believed about myself was being exaggerated in my own mind. My thoughts and the "tapes" I played in my head kept me locked in a type of prison. The messages kept repeating themselves, telling me I wasn't good enough and that I wasn't smart enough; I wasn't going to amount to much. What I have realized is by journaling and refuting is that those messages aren't true. I am good enough and smart enough, and now I am starting to believe it.[48]

A senior leader reported that he felt like he was gaining clarity and power over his thought life:

I feel like a new man. I still struggle, but I don't feel stuck in my thinking. When I find myself drifting back to negativity, I now have tools and a process to take back control. My wife commented to me the other day that she noticed how upbeat and positive I have become. In fact, she said, I am a much better listener. Wow, I didn't realize how negative I was, and it all starts with my own internal thoughts.[49]

Will you join those who are taking control of negative thinking patterns through this simple sixty-day challenge to observe, log, and refute? You, too, can experience the transformational mind-renewal process. You can take control of your thinking, which begins with inhibiting negative patterns that may be subtle or unconscious, but over time, each thought does add up.

In the next chapter, we will unpack a method I have developed from my study, research, and teaching on habit development. This method has helped me and those involved in our training sessions to learn the process of effective and successful transformational habits that can unleash your "sweet spot" of personal greatness.

Questions for Reflection

1. Are you stuck in negative thought patterns?
2. Do you believe you can take control of your negative thought patterns?
3. Are you willing to engage in the "Observe, log, and refute sixty-day challenge"?
4. If so, when will you begin, and do you have an accountability partner or group to support you in the process?

Steps for Action

1. Engage in the "Observe, log, and refute sixty-day challenge" as outlined in this chapter.
2. What negative thinking patterns emerge, and how are you reframing those patterns?
3. Have an accountability partner check on your progress weekly or bi-weekly during the sixty-days.

CHAPTER 19

THE HEAD OF A SERVANT LEADER: HABIT MODEL— TRAIN: THE 4R MODEL APPROACH

> *A lifetime of habits ingrained by repetition can seemingly make us slaves to a not always beneficial master—our own brain.*
> —JEFFERY SCHWARTZ AND REBECCA GLADDING, *YOU ARE NOT YOUR BRAIN*

Do you feel like you are stuck in "Groundhog Day"? The 1993 movie *Groundhog Day*, starring Bill Murray, portrayed a man stuck in the same day over and over. Nothing changes as much as he wants it to, and everything is very predictable. Many of us are like this character; we want to change our lifestyles, our mind-sets, and our habits, but we, too, are stuck in the trap of "Groundhog Day."

Left to its own devices, your mind can cause you to believe things that are not true and to act in any number of self-destructive ways. As we have seen in the previous chapter, when we believe toxic and deceptive brain messages, we go to places—mentally and emotionally—where we don't want to be and find ourselves acting in ways that aren't congruent with our hearts or doing things we really don't want to do.

Toxic thinking is deceptive, and we may believe and act in a number of ways:

- *Overthinking problems and fretting over things that are out of our control*
- *Getting stuck or panicked by unfounded fears and worries*
- *Blaming and chastising ourselves for things that are not our fault*
- *Engaging in unhealthy behaviors to escape life's daily stresses*
- *Reverting to past patterns when trying to make a change*

Do any of these sound familiar to you? The more often you act in unhealthy ways of thinking, the more you teach your brain that what is simply a habit (a learned behavior) is essential to your survival. Your brain does not distinguish between whether the action is beneficial or destructive; it just responds to how you behave and then generates strong impulses, thoughts, desires, cravings, and urges that compel you to perpetuate your habit, whatever it may be. Unfortunately, more often than not, these behaviors and patterns are not the ones that improve your life.

The good news is that you can overcome the brain's controls and rewire your brain to work for you by learning to renew your mind and thinking, debunking the myths and lies it has been so successfully selling you, and choosing to act in healthy ways.

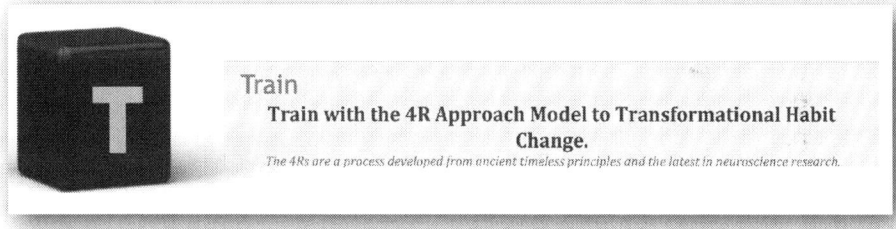

Train

Train with the 4R Approach Model to Transformational Habit Change.

The 4Rs are a process developed from ancient timeless principles and the latest in neuroscience research.

The 4R Model Approach to transformational change teaches simple skills based on ancient wisdom and the latest research in neuroscience. These skills can be used and put to practice every day and can literally transform and renew your thinking, habits, and mind-set. I am thankful for the research and work of Dr. Jeffery Schwartz at UCLA. His groundbreaking work with those with obsessive-compulsive disorder (OCD) has reinforced the strong belief that the mind can change the brain, referred to as *neuroplasticity*. His book *Brain Lock, written with Beverly Beyette* and *You*

Are Not Your Brain, coatuthored with Rebecca Gladding, MD, have been instrumental in helping people to thrive by overcoming their thought patterns, such as: excessive nervousness, worry and anxiety, tension, depression, anger, substance abuse, and other addictions, habits, and automatic behaviors. This work goes along with breakthrough research in self-directed neuroplasticity, the belief that the brain can change and heal if you take control over your responses to negative thinking patterns and understand how your brain works. As stated by Norm Doidge,

> *The discovery that our thoughts can change the structure and function of our brains, even into old age, is one of the most important breakthroughs in four centuries. The common wisdom was that after childhood the brain changed only when it began the long process of decline; that when the brain cells failed to develop properly, or were injured, or died, they could not be replaced. Nor could the brain alter its structure and find a new way to function if part of it was damaged. The idea that the brain can change its own structure and function through thought and activity is, I believe, the most important alteration in our view of the brain since we first sketched out its basic anatomy and the working of its basic component, the neuron.*[50]

Habits (good and bad) are what we create when we do something over and over, to the point where we no longer need to think about it consciously in order to repeat the process perfectly. This applies not only to things we do physically but also to our thoughts. When we think the same thing over and over, it becomes a habit of thought. A habit of thought over time becomes an attitude or belief. There is nothing as powerful as attitude. Attitudes dictate our responses to the present and determine the quality of our future. *Attitude can simply be defined as our mind-set or mental conditioning that determines our interpretation of and response to our environment.* It is our way of thinking. Attitude is a natural product of the integration of self-worth, self-concept, self-esteem, and sense of value or significance. In essence, attitude is the manifestation of who we think we are. We live our lives based on who we think we are.

In order for change or transformation to happen, the urgency level must be high, and the need or desire must be compelling and realistic for the individual.

THE HEART, HEAD, AND HANDS OF A SERVANT LEADER

In other words, the urgency level must be strong enough to motivate your nonconscious mind (heart) to commit to action that will ultimately affect your conscious choices. *Most of us can't break certain habits or create new ones because we don't have the right thoughts and attitudes that will enable us to change.* Our convictions determine what is stored in our hearts, and the heart is the container of attitude. It is like a bank account that we draw from that determines the way we live our lives. We become what we learn, listen to, see, hear, and experience. *Your nonconscious mind, or heart, attitude affects your conscious perceptions and mind-set.* In other words, the height to which your heart aspires depends on the information that is in it. We will never rise above our mental conditioning or the bar that we have set for ourselves. **We can be our own worst enemies or our greatest allies.** Your perspective is shaped by your internal belief system, and your internal belief system will take on either a victim's mentality or a victor's mentality. Whatever is stored in your heart determines how highly or how lowly you think about yourself and what you believe you can accomplish.

The **4R Model Approach** gives you a framework for understanding the process of how habits are formed and developed, and you can then learn how to focus your attention in beneficial ways so that you can retrain and renew your mind, habits, and thinking. Let's look at an overview of the four steps.

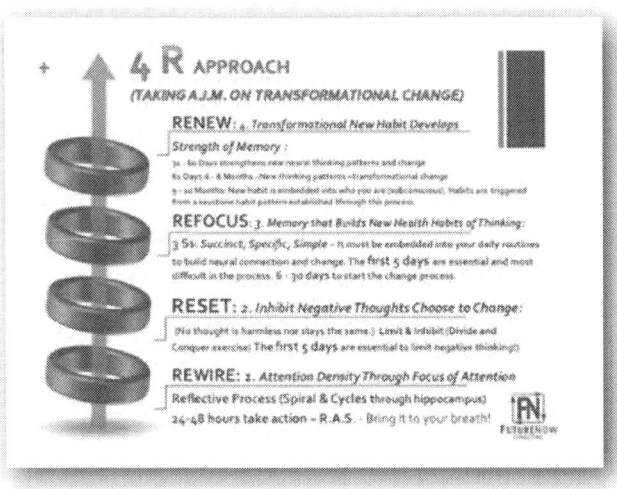

The first step is **Rewire**—identifying the thought, habit, emotion, or behavior through focused, reflective attention. The next step is **Reset**—recognizing that no thought or habit is harmless. You must choose to change and inhibit the negative thoughts. realizing the intensity and/or interference of negative thinking on new thoughts or building positive habits. The third step is **Refocus**—focusing attention on the "new" desired thought, habit, emotion, or behavior, which builds positive memory that is embedded into your daily routines. The fourth step is **Renew**—the process of new habit development is based on developing the "strength of memory" over time; new thinking patterns over time = transformation.

Step 1: Rewire

The process begins with identifying your **"it,"** what needs to be changed or developed, and focusing your mental process by paying attention and engaging in reflection. Dr. Schwartz and physicist Dr. Henry Stapp linked what is called the *Quantum Zeno Effect (QZE)* with what happens when close attention is paid to a mental experience:

> *The mental act of focusing attention stabilizes the associated brain circuits. Concentrating attention on your mental experience, whether a thought, an insight, a picture in your mind's eye, or a fear, maintains the brain state arising in association with that experience. Over time, paying enough attention to any specific brain connection keeps the relevant circuitry open and dynamically alive.*[51]

Thus, QZE eventually hardwires and makes physical changes in the brain's structure or creates a habit or a new mental map. Simply, whatever we intentionally and purposely focus our attention upon, we become. One of the simplest ways to bring focus of attention is through breathing. In Chapter 14, we talked about the how the RAS system in your brain filters the incoming information and affects what you pay attention to, how aroused you are, and what is not going to get access to all of your brain. It is the key that turns the brain on or off, more or less, although, as mentioned, it would be better to say it is the key that turns the brain and the body up or down. **Deep breathing activates and/or controls the RAS**, because the *breath* and the *body* are interconnected. The first step of the rewiring process is to focus your attention on your "it."

The **first twenty-four to forty-eight hours** will be essential to the process of developing the sense of urgency and strength of desire and motivation to rewire your habits. As you focus and reflect on your "it," your mind and brain take that thought, idea, or concept and begin to grasp it—to literally take hold of it. As you grasp it, you begin to have clarity and are now consciously aware of it as it cycles through your memory system in your brain. The hippocampus is the structure in the brain that acts as a sort of clearinghouse for thoughts. It classifies incoming information as either having short- or long-term importance and "files" it accordingly, converting temporary thoughts into permanent thoughts that become a part of you. Thus, in order for a thought or habit to get filed as a permanent thought or habit that becomes a part of you, you have to **own it or choose to take a specific action**. It cycles through your hippocampus for about twenty-four to forty-eight hours, and the longer it spirals and cycles without active choice, the more it loses the sense of urgency and strength of desire or motivation. In other words, **if you don't grasp it and choose to do something with it, you lose it.** The strength of clarity diminishes if you don't act upon it and take action to keep it.

Step 2: Reset

In the previous chapter, we discussed the importance of being a "gatekeeper" of negative thinking. Negative thinking patterns have a profound effect on the way we think and live. Step 2 is like hitting the reset button in your brain and thinking by inhibiting negative thinking. We highlighted how you can reverse the effects of the "it can't be done" virus and learned helplessness default thinking. As noted, even if you are consumed by toxic thinking because of one or both of these patterns or live in a toxic environment that is discouraging, you can take control of your thought life. You can break the chains that have been limiting your development into your unique personal "sweet spot" of greatness.

It the Reset phase, research indicates how important the **first five days** are for inhibiting negative thinking patterns. There is no such thing as a harmless thought, so we need to guard and be the gatekeepers of our thoughts and emotions. Dr. Caroline Leaf states:

> *Detoxifying your thoughts can be like selecting a book from a shelf in your library of memories, rewriting a page in that book, then placing back on the shelf free of toxic thoughts and emotions. The good news is we can change those pathways within four days and create new ones within twenty-one days.*[52]

I believe that the internal process of inhibiting negative or toxic thoughts in the first five days of clarity, as well as developing a plan around your "it," are absolutely essential to building new positive habits that will empower you and cause you to thrive.

Step 3: Refocus

Although we are using a linear, stepwise model, this whole process is very integrated and can happen simultaneously. In the Refocus step, you refocus your attention on building memories that build new, healthy habits of thinking. I have created a memory device to help you grasp this new habit or way of thinking. I call it the 3Ss.

The 3Ss

Simple: We know that in order for us to remember anything, we have to keep it simple. If we take something that is complex and break it down to make it simple, we will remember it. When you are dealing with habit development, remember that genius is found in simplicity.

Succinct: The habit shouldn't be too detailed, but it must give enough trigger words for you to remember and focus on it. This may be one of the most difficult things for you to do, narrowing it down to the most important information in order to build a positive memory habit.

Specific: It must be embedded into your daily routines in very specific ways. The more specific and applied it is in your daily routines, the more powerful will be the building of a transformational healthy thinking habit.

For example, I struggled most of my life with self-doubt, as I shared in Chapter 6. Let me now share how I used the **3Ss** to overcome self-doubt. I decided through the rewiring process that this pattern of thinking began when a significant person in my life said that I was never going to amount to much. To reset and inhibit the negative thinking patterns and learned helplessness in regard to self-doubt, I decided to focus on what I was gifted to be and do—like my teacher Mrs. Rumble told me as a child, "I see greatness in you."

I came up with something that was *simple, succinct,* and *specific* for me. I was no longer going to allow the negative "tapes" of self-doubt to enter into my thinking. In order to make it simple and succinct, I created an index card with this sentence: *I have been created for greatness, and I have been given all I need to accomplish that greatness today!* My problem was that I just didn't believe the message that Mrs. Rumble had spoken to me when I was a child, and I chose to believe the message of self-doubt I had overheard from my father. So I determined that every day for thirty days, I was going to review that card with my new mind-set thinking, and every time the seeds of self-doubt started to sprout in my thinking, I would pull out the card and review it.

I have to admit that it was difficult those first few days. In fact, I started to second-guess myself and even initiated the internal talk that I could never really change: *Who are you to be great; you are never going to amount to much.* In this process, you are literally fighting a battle for your mind, and you lose when you choose to believe a message that is not true of you. However, at about the sixth day, the message and mind-set started to feel more like a fit for me. From that day through the thirtieth day, I saw myself becoming more consistent in believing the statement and using the card when the negative tapes started playing. I had begun the process of transformational thinking that was leading me into my own "sweet spot" of personal greatness.

Step 4: Renewal

The question most often asked regarding transformational thinking and habit change is: *How long will it take?* The answer is: *That depends on you.* The research indicates that it begins just like I outlined in this chapter. However, mind-set change is a process of rewiring and birthing a new way of thinking, and that depends on several factors: the strength of the old habits or old ways of thinking; the intensity of the desire and motivation to change; the self-discipline and focus of attention of the individual; how simple, succinct, and specific the new habit is; and a person's willingness to go through the battle and pain of fighting the toxic or negative thinking that is holding him or her back.

Typically, you can see **initial habit change in the first thirty to sixty days**; however, for the process of strength of memory for the new habit of thinking to be part of you, **sixty-one days or nine to ten months is a better estimate**. One of the reasons people don't see a renewed mind that helps them tap into their unique personal greatness is that they don't stick with the habit long enough. I don't know how it is for you, but change for me can happen very quickly. However, in order for it to become part of who I am—or, put another way, to unleash my true potential and greatness—it is a process that takes place over time.

I have used the 4R Model Approach in training sessions, coaching, and teaching. I have also taught the process as a development tool and as a framework for coaching and leading others.

A senior-level leader commented:

> *This process [4R Approach] has given me a handle on how to change and understand why change is so hard for me and others. It has given me a mental framework to help me to be more successful in my personal growth and development.*[53]

A graduate student and educational administrator claimed:

> *The 4R Approach has improved my focus on what really matters in the moment, right now. I have been using this approach for the past sixty days, and it has helped me personally to work through the process of breaking the habit of talking way too much and not listening. I am hearing more and asking more questions, and in turn, I am more in tune to people around me. In fact, my husband commented to me that he felt like I was listening and really hearing what he was saying. Wow, I guess I did talk too much.*[54]

A middle-level leader has been using the 4R Approach to work with his direct reports and team:

> *I have seen the results in my own life and wanted to use this process in my one-on-one and team meetings. Over the past sixty days, my one-on-one meetings have moved from information to connecting with what is most important to that individual in the moment. I help them focus on one area and walk them through, making it* **simple, succinct, and specific.** *They come back to me with their plan in twenty-four to forty-eight hours, and I try to send them a note or e-mail in the first five days to ask how they are doing with the process. This gives me the opportunity in our one-on-one follow-ups to focus on what they are working on and help them with accountability. In our team meetings, an e-mail is sent at least forty-eight hours before the meeting and asks them to put down what one thing is most important for us to accomplish in this meeting. Then, someone on the team takes that input and sorts and prioritizes it for the meeting. (We try to narrow it to one to five items, depending on the scope.) After the meeting, each person is assigned a next step, and everyone has to report back to the team within five days on what has been done to that point.*

Then, when we have our biweekly meeting, there is a focus, and each person has ownership of the process. So far, there has been a tremendous response from my team, and they seem to be more engaged as a result.[55]

Questions for Reflection

1. How will you use the 4R Approach in your personal growth and development?
2. If you have struggled with habit development, what part of the 4R Approach will be most helpful in assisting you to transform your thinking?
3. How would you use the 4R Approach in coaching others?

Steps for Action

1. Apply the 4R Approach and process in an area of your work environment, such as meetings or training sessions.
2. Apply the 4R Approach and process in an area of your personal life.

CHAPTER 20

THE HANDS OF A SERVANT LEADER: BALANCING CARE AND CANDOR

> *People don't care how much you know until they know how much you care.*
> —JOHN MAXWELL

Part of the deep work of becoming a servant leader involves becoming aware of, and in some cases changing, very deeply ingrained patterns in the ways you interact with others. A leader can be extremely disciplined, focused, and goal-oriented, but without interpersonal connection, he or she will probably fail. We were created for connection, relationship, and meaningful interaction. Central to the heart mission of servant leadership is to focus consciously on those human qualities of connecting that are the guts and emotion of leadership. The actions and behaviors of a servant leader must strike a unique balance of between **caring and candor**.

MICHAEL J. STABILE, PHD

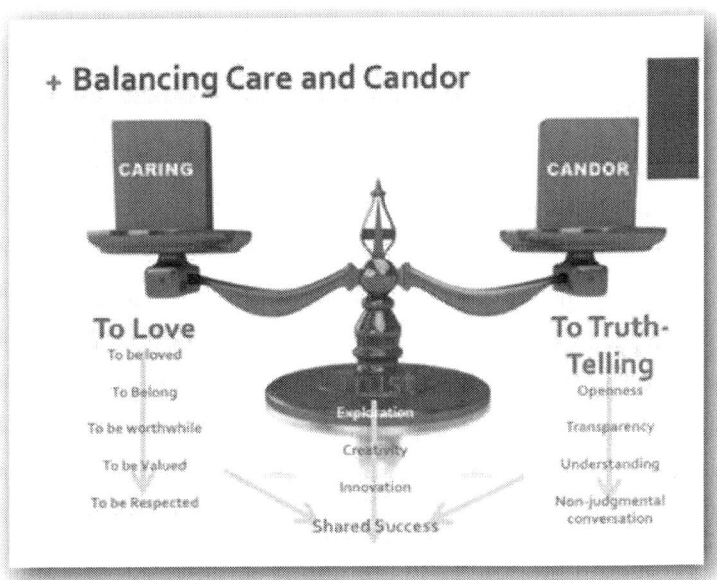

The "caring" part of care and candor is often neglected in our interactions, especially in our public lives. I define *interpersonal connection* as a form of synergy that facilitates an attachment, which creates more physical, emotional, intellectual, and/or spiritual energy than the person or people involved could generate independently. Caring involves connecting with the deepest and most primal need of humanity—to love and be loved. We were created for love: to feel loved, to belong or be included, to sense that we are worthy of unconditional love, to be valued by others, and to be respected. You don't necessarily need to touch another person physically or hug someone to produce this **caring effect**. Instead, you can touch someone's heart with words of sympathy or support, or you can validate someone's concern and trigger a more positive mental and physical state of mind. "Life and death are found in the power of the tongue." Our words matter, and understanding how powerful language is to interpersonal connection and interaction is a skill that must be progressively mastered and practiced in our daily interactions at home, work, and play.

Ancient wisdom and modern neuroscience tell us that we were created for connection and community. Matthew Lieberman, a professor, researcher, and writer, and one of the founders of the relatively new field of study involving social cognitive and affective neuroscience, writes:

> *Food, water, and shelter are not the most basic needs for (human beings). Instead, being socially connected and cared for is a need with a capital N. Love and belonging might seem like a convenience we can live without, but our biology is built to thirst for connection because it is linked to our most basic survival needs...but our need for connection is the bedrock upon which the others are built.*[56]

Dr. Lieberman and his wife, psychologist Naomi Eisenberger, have been studying the power of social pain. Their research has demonstrated that social rejection or lack of connection is just as painful as physical pain. They have done this by showing that the same regions of the brain that are affected by physical pain are also activated when a person feels disconnected, rejected, unheard, excluded, disrespected, devalued, or treated unfairly:

> *Our basic findings linking social exclusion to [specific brain regions] have been replicated in a number of studies and extended to people experiencing grief over the death of a loved one, remembering a recent romantic breakup, being negatively evaluated, and just looking at disapproving faces...Throughout our lives, we are destined to experience different forms of social rejection and loss...But it requires us to pay for it with possibility of pain, real pain, every time we connect with another human being who has the power to leave us or withhold love.*[57]

As we have seen in previous chapters, who we are is very ingrained in our mind-sets. Some of those patterns are reflected in the way we connect with people. Connecting with others also involves picking up on the "signals" they are sending about themselves, their emotions, and their needs. Signals are the verbal and nonverbal messages that confirm or deny the truth of a person's communications. Most signals are subtle. Sometimes signals are conscious—sometimes, unconscious. However, the power of connection between and among human beings as illustrated through

Lieberman's research brings to the forefront the foundational **"why"** behind a servant leader's focus on intentional caring.

George Kohlrieser and colleagues in their book *Care to Dare* give four main sources of human signals that are part of the verbal or nonverbal exchanges between people:[58]

- *Body:* Body language includes gestures, posture, facial expressions, and tone of voice. These can be conscious or unconscious, positive or negative.
- *Emotions:* Examples of basic emotions are anger, fear, joy, sadness, disgust, and surprise. These emotions activate the body, which in turn sends out signals.
- *Mind:* You send signals about what is going on in your mind. What you think becomes a signal, often (but not always) through the words that you use. What you believe about the other person affects the signals you send.
- *Spirit:* Spirit indicates the intention that is behind all other signals: your purpose, your motivation while you are taking action, and your end goal. Signals from the spirit convey a sense of judgment.

One manifestation of connection is the ability to feel empathy and compassion for the other person. **A common misconception is that connection equals friendship.** You do not necessarily have to like someone to connect with him or her. You only need a **common goal**. For example, in work situations, there may be certain people you have to work with, but you are not going to be friends with them for whatever reason. If we allow a mind-set of *connection = friendship*, then we may unconsciously be giving signals of rejection or exclusion either physically, emotionally, mentally, or spiritually.

Our brains have a friend-or-foe "early-warning system," a flashlight that changes focus based on very quick judgments about whether someone is a friend, and therefore treated fairly, or whether they are a foe, and therefore treated with suspicion. When the foe system is alerted by a perceived sense of threat, people will shut down, become distant, and focus on problems as they attempt to reduce the perceived danger. As we have seen in this chapter, our perception of others as friend, foe, or neutral trigger signals that others pick up, sense, and feel. People are fundamentally motivated by a sense of belonging. When people say, "I feel hurt," they really do feel the pain.

In our Servant Leadership Coaching System training process, we use an online assessment tool called the Servant Leadership Assessment Process for Caring Leadership. This assessment uses the acronym SERVANTS to conceptualize caring leadership in action in all areas of life. As noted in the chapter-opening quote, "People don't care how much you know until they know how much you care." Care is an intentional action in your formal and informal interactions with people. It helps leaders self-evaluate and gather input and feedback from direct reports and supervisors. They receive a customized report that graphically represents the data and can be used as a reflective coaching tool, along with questions to ask about what the data mean.

The behaviors of servant leaders are clear, practical and learnable. In fact, you may already be exhibiting some of the eight characteristics represented by the SERVANTS acronym:

S—Self-Control (patience with self and others or "impulse" control): A servant leader remains composed and dependable, especially when under pressure. This characteristic is so fundamental that a leader needs to master it before he or she is able to portray other characteristics.

E—Encouragement (to give others attention, appreciation, and common courtesy through kindness): Servant leaders are good at directing the mind-set of other people to focus on the positive rather than the negative. They know and understand the power of the accelerator habit of appreciation and encouragement. Attention, appreciation, encouragement, and recognition are key internal motivators that are part of unleashing personal greatness. Giving encouragement helps others to see their potential and the opportunity for learning, even in a crisis or time of difficulty.

***R*—Respect (to treat others as important and give them dignity):** When you give genuine respect, people sense and believe that you are present in the moment and holistically accessible and available rather than detached and unavailable or "too busy." What is important is the perception that **you are available if needed**. When you intentionally and habitually focus your attention on giving others the respect they long for and are drawn to, not out of obligation, there is a heartfelt connection and interaction.

V—Value (by meeting the legitimate needs of others, not their wants): Servant leaders accept individuals for who they are. They show caring for the human being before focusing on the issue or problem by separating the person from the problem. As far as possible, they avoid judging and criticizing people. However, this characteristic goes beyond acceptance and beyond seeing the potential. It takes those concepts into direct action. Servant leaders actively dare people to unleash their potential and personal greatness by providing tangible opportunities for risk taking.

A—Authentic (to be authentic [literally, humility—to be the "true" you], not arrogant, boastful, or prideful): To be authentic is to build your legitimacy through honest relationships with others and value their input. Generally, authentic leaders are positive people with truthful self-concepts who promote openness. By building trust and generating enthusiastic support from others, authentic leaders are able to improve individual and organizational performance. When humility is the ultimate self-confidence, a leader is not afraid of not knowing the answer. Not knowing an answer is an opportunity for mutual discovery and growth, not an indictment of a leader's performance. When humility is the ultimate self-confidence, a leader is not concerned with receiving credit or acclaim.

N—Never hold resentment (when wrong or wronged, forgiving and not holding grudges): Forgiveness is letting go of a false sense of power in exchange for real power. Thus, forgiveness has little, if anything, to do with the person who hurt or betrayed us. It is purely an internal matter. To forgive, we go inside to consciously make any necessary changes in what we think and believe about a person or situation, and we embrace new ways of thinking that allow us to reclaim our power to express freely the essence of who we are. It is a *choice* that we have the ability to make in present moments of decision.

T—Trustworthy (to be honest and free from deceptive behavior): Your trust as a leader is earned and maintained by the consistency you exhibit as you go through various tests over time. Therefore, a servant leader must be tested to see if he or she can stand up under pressure. If you want to be trustworthy, you must learn that character is built through tests over time and that integrity involves the integration of your thoughts, words, and actions. Consistency in our behavior over time is the key to being trustworthy. (See Chapter 11 for more on being trustworthy.)

S2—Stick to your commitments (sticking to the choice[s] you have made): It is often tempting to give up. It's easy to lose focus. Distractions are everywhere. Pressing on in the face of strong opposition or demoralizing apathy is no fun. Self-discipline is never easy, but forcing yourself to keep your commitments when others are backsliding means you have to proceed on emergency power. **Don't misunderstand:** *Leaders don't keep doing things that are not working. They just try something else.* When that doesn't work, they try something else again. Leaders regularly change what they are doing, but they **never quit doing something**.

The "Candor" Part of Care and Candor

To lead successfully, it is important for you to value people. That is foundational to solid relationships. Caring for others demonstrates that you value and respect them. However, if you want to help them get better, you have to be honest about where they need to improve. That shows that you value the person's potential, and it requires candor. There is sometimes a misunderstanding of servant leadership as being "soft," or the kindly parental figure who just hugs you and tells you everything is great.

In my experience, all of us need someone to come alongside us to help us improve. As a leader, it is your **responsibility** and your **privilege** to be the person who helps others get better. That often begins with a candid conversation. I believe that people can improve their attitudes and their abilities. And because I do, I talk to them about where they're coming up short. If you're a leader and you want to help serve people, then you need to be willing to have those difficult conversations. With that in mind, let's examine the cost of **not balancing caring and candor**.

First, if you care without candor, it creates dysfunctional relationships. Over time, a relationship that has just focused on the caring component of support without the transparency, honesty, and truth-telling sets up a dysfunctional dependency. When you avoid hard or difficult conversations, you are missing the opportunity to challenge individuals appropriately or prepare or fortify them for life in the larger world.

Second, you could develop a **codependency**. Codependency means that one or both people in a relationship are making the dysfunction of the relationship more important than anything else. A classic codependent relationship involves someone who is hopelessly entangled with a partner who is out of control through alcoholism, addiction, or violent behavior; but the term has been more recently used to mean anyone who feels dependent, helpless, and out of control in a relationship, or someone who is unable to leave an unsatisfying, toxic, or abusive one. A relationship that becomes codependent contains unhealthy interactions, and it does not enhance the lives of the people involved. People in these relationships are not taking responsibility for making their own lives or the relationship work.

Third, it can lead to **toxic relationships or environments** that can be mentally, emotionally, spiritually, or physically harmful to some or all of the participants. Although codependent relationships can also be toxic relationships, the term *toxic* is usually used to refer to the more abusive varieties. The following may be indicators of a toxic relationship or environment:

- *It may seem like you can't do anything right:* You feel like you are not good enough or make others feel like they are not good enough. As a result, you or others may become defensive and feel ashamed, inadequate, or judged.
- *Everything is about them and never about you:* You have feelings too, but the other person or persons won't hear them. You're unable to have a two-sided conversation where your opinion is heard, considered, and respected. Instead of acknowledging your feelings, they battle with you until they get the last word.
- *You find yourself unable to enjoy good moments with toxic individuals:* Every day brings another challenge. It seems as though they are always raising gripes or criticisms about you.
- *You're uncomfortable being yourself around that person or in that environment:* You don't feel free to speak your mind. You have to put on a different face just to be accepted by that person or group. You realize that you don't even recognize yourself anymore.
- *You're not allowed to grow and change:* Whenever you aim to grow and improve yourself, the others involved respond with mockery and disbelief. There is no encouragement or support for your efforts. Instead, they keep you stuck in old judgments, insisting that you will never be any different than you are now.

The degree of dysfunction, codependency, or toxicity in relationships can vary. Most of us get a little dependent, and therefore dysfunctional, from time to time—especially when we're tired, stressed, or otherwise overloaded. What makes the difference between this normal, occasional human frailty and true dysfunction is our ability to recognize, confront, and correct dysfunction when it happens in our relationships.

But care balanced with candor creates developing relationships. When you combine **caring and candor,** you have a winning combination of success. The people you serve are looking forward to your insightful conversations, and they know you are acting in their best interests. Meaningful relationships are defined by how people care about one another as they share a common bond that allows each person to become the best he or she can be.

When you practice candor, it demonstrates leadership abilities. It shows that you can address tough issues and challenges in a caring way. Caring means taking prudent action and maintaining integrity by having a timely, open conversation with the person before a problem escalates out of control and has a negative impact on the family, business, or culture.

In the next chapter, we will focus on how to engage in healthy conflict through candor. As a servant leader, what you say can make a large deposit in trust. Under most circumstances, the trust balance with people is the result of numerous small deposits. You must want an unstoppable flow of ideas, open debate, and constructive conflict. To cultivate a culture of candor, you have to be a role model for candor in an exaggerated way. **Talk about it. Teach its value. Praise it. Most of all, reward it.**

Questions for Reflection

1. How are you doing in balancing caring and candor?
2. Using the SERVANTS acronym as a reflective tool, what areas do you feel are your greatest strengths, and what areas need improvement?
3. Are candor and healthy conflict in balance in your relationships?
5. Are your relationships and environment being affected because of a lack of candor?

Steps for Action

1. Ask significant people in your life how you are doing in the area of caring leadership.
2. What are you going to do with the feedback you received/
3. What area will you focus on for at least thirty days?

CHAPTER 21

THE HANDS OF A SERVANT LEADER: ENGAGE IN HEALTHY CONFLICT

> *When there is trust, conflict becomes nothing but the pursuit of truth, an attempt to find the best possible answer.*
> —PATRICK LENCIONI, *THE ADVANTAGE*

Contrary to popular wisdom and behavior, conflict is not a bad thing. In fact, the fear of conflict is almost always a sign of problems. However, when you understand the importance of conflict, it is much easier to engage in it. A servant leader's ability to personally model appropriate conflict behavior is essential. Avoiding conflict when it is necessary and productive may create, allow, and even encourage this dysfunction to thrive.

Many people prefer to avoid conflict. There are a variety of reasons for this, including the need to be liked, the pursuit of acceptance, past negative experiences, and the desire for stability in one's life. Unfortunately, servant leaders cannot lead effectively without addressing conflict as it arises. In fact, if they choose to avoid conflict at all costs, they can put their relationships or organizations at great risk. Personal conflict competence is an essential individual skill, but to gain the full benefit of it, you need to expand the use of this skill. To be credible, leaders have to improve their own skill sets. They must be able to demonstrate control of their emotions and model the use of constructive conflict behaviors.

They should also coach and mentor others to help them improve in these crucial areas.

How does a person go about developing the ability and willingness to engage in healthy conflict and have difficult conversations and/or meetings? The first step is to acknowledge that conflict is productive and that you may have a tendency to avoid it. As long as you believe that conflict is unnecessary or have a fear of it, there is little chance that it will occur in a healthy or productive way. But beyond mere recognition, here we discuss a simple model for making conflict more common and productive: the *LEARNS model*.

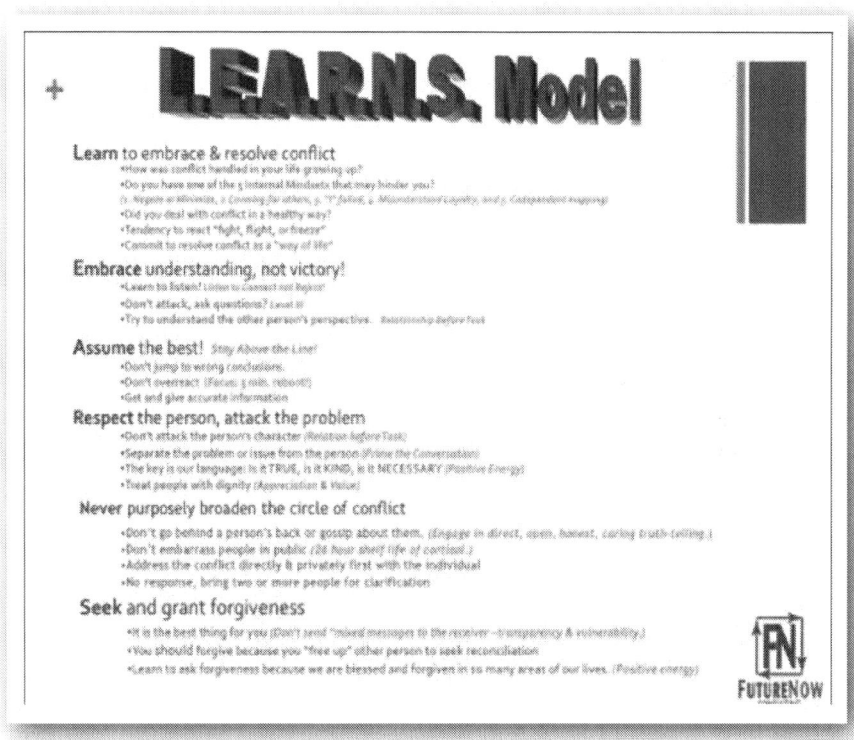

The LEARNS Model for Engaging in Healthy Conflict

The LEARNS model was created to help you to reframe thinking about conflict and to provide a simple process for cultivating a shift in mind-set.

Leaders who can learn to respond to difficult conversations in an effective manner and in the right way will discover that solving conflict results in improvement in both personal and professional relationships. Following the process will ensure that you handle tough conversations more skillfully and reduce stress for all involved.

Learn to **embrace and resolve** conflict:

Ask yourself: *How was conflict handled in your life when you were growing up? Did you deal with conflict in a healthy way? Do you have one of the following five internal mind-sets that may hinder you?*

Five Internal Mind-Sets That Hinder "Difficult" Conversations

1. **Abnormally high pain threshold:** You have developed coping skills to negate, minimize, or put up with unhealthy conflict or toxic behavior.
2. **Covering for others:** You avoid conflict or difficult conversations because you are just "too nice" and don't want to cause friction or problems. On the other hand, you may have taken on the burden and responsibility for another person or group of people and don't want them to get in trouble or cause issues.
3. **Believing that engaging in conflict will end the relationship:** You may feel that if you do engage in conflict or have a difficult conversation, either the relationship has or will fail or that you personally have failed.
4. **Misunderstood loyalty:** As in covering for others, you have a misplaced responsibility for another, and as a result, you have placed a higher value on loyalty than on confronting the truth and risking the relationship.
5. **Codependent mapping:** You are enabling the dysfunctional or toxic behavior or situation because you are only telling people what they want to hear. Instead of empowering others with the

truth or open candor, you avoid and reinforce their thinking or "bad" behavior, habits, or lifestyle.

These five internal mind-sets may be keys to helping you understand why you have difficulty engaging in conflict. Take time to reflect and see if any of these five are ingrained in your thinking and affecting your ability to have difficult conversations.

By addressing the situation as soon as possible and not avoiding it for whatever reason, we learn to embrace and resolve conflict. Difficult conversations that are left to fester do not get any easier to handle. In fact, you'll only waste time and energy deciding how you will handle the conversation. In many cases, we become anxious if a difficult topic is not addressed, which can lead to unnecessary negativity and stress and result in more unnecessary conflict.

Embrace understanding, not victory!

Difficult conversations can quite easily lead to conflict if they are not addressed carefully and sensitively. But instead of going in full guns blazing and focusing on the areas of difference, start off by focusing on the successful aspects of your relationship, because this approach will create a positive atmosphere for your conversation.

In Chapter 17 we examined the power of connection through empathy. When we establish a connection with others, especially in a difficult conversation, it always begins with a heart mind-set of understanding from another point of view. Focus on relationship instead of on who or what is right. One of the biggest mistakes I have made in having difficult conversations is focusing on being right or winning the battle. Therefore, **don't attack; ask questions** that help you to understand the point of view of the other person or group. Asking questions that are not biased or leading and that don't force them to come to your conclusion opens up the conversational space, because there is a sense by the other person or group that you are really listening and want to hear what they feel and think.

Assume the best! *Stay above the Line!*

Accept responsibility for your role; this is part of being an exceptional leader. To accept responsibility for your side in things means that you take personal responsibility when you have jumped to the wrong conclusions, said or acted in an offensive or "wrong" way, or neglected to provide enough information or the necessary guidance. We all have a tendency to overact. I can blame this on my Italian temper, or I can take responsibility for my actions and behavior. We need to stop blaming, pointing the finger, and accusing others; see it, own it, solve it, and take the right actions to engage in healthy conflict. Make sure that you are **getting and giving accurate information** about the person or situation.

Take time to reboot your thinking and emotions before engaging in a difficult conversation. Make sure your heart and mind stay above the line and that you do not drop below it in the heat of a difficult conversation.

Respect the person; attack the problem!

The temptation in difficult conversations is to **defend and protect. Don't attack the person's character.** Always be respectful of others, no matter how they have treated you, behaved, or what they have said. I know that this is easier said than done, but in separating the problem or issue from the person, you open up the conversational space and disarm the emotions that are so easily triggered.

The key is in our language. Remember that language is more than just your words; it's your affect, your body language, and your tone of voice. In having a difficult conversation, it is **not about who is right**; it is about finding the **truth**. In order to get to the truth, you must be willing to let go of your preconceived ideas, feelings, and impressions and explore all sides of the story. You first have to **understand before you can be understood**. Be kind, and speak only when necessary. When you treat people with dignity**,** you will see a tremendous shift in their attitude and body language.

Never purposely broaden the circle of conflict!

Ancient wisdom and common sense give us some guidelines. First, **don't go behind a person's back or gossip** about someone. Gossip has become socially acceptable in many settings and cultures. I know most people don't consider it to be gossip when you simply talk to people who agree with you about the shortcomings of others. But no matter how you dress it up, it is still **gossip!** Gossip is the fuel for the fire of misunderstandings, hurt feelings, and disharmony. Here is a simple definition for gossip: *Sharing the negative about a person or situation to others who cannot or will not solve the problem.*

Second, **don't embarrass people in public**—no matter how right you think you are in doing it. You are only asking for a battle or war, depending on the person. No one likes to be **put down in front of others**. Our goal is **not to destroy or embitter**, but to **restore, forgive, and uplift**.

Third, when having a difficult conversation, address the conflict **directly and privately first** with the individual. The circle of conflict is like a forest fire; it starts out small, but it broadens if left unchecked. Keep the circle of conflict small, and don't allow it to get out of hand. When you avoid direct and private confrontation, you are revealing more about your character, fears, and internal hindrances. Go directly to the problem or issue. As much as possible, deal with misunderstandings, conflicts, and disagreements as soon as you possibly can. My experience is that that the longer you wait, the more the circle of conflict has the opportunity to get out of control. Make it a practice to deal with conflicts in **twenty-four hours or less**. Sometimes that means within minutes!

Seek and grant forgiveness!

Begin with the end in mind: What is your ultimate goal in having a difficult conversation? Ultimately, the heart of a servant leader is focused on the relationship, and if that is foundational, then when there is conflict, misunderstanding, hurt, or offense, it is the moral responsibility of the servant leader to seek and grant forgiveness. Ultimately, this is the best thing for you, because unresolved conflict leads to all kinds of trouble, both internally with your conscience and externally in regard to relationships. We are called to live in harmony and peace with others as much as we possibly can.

You should forgive others, because when you do, you **"free up"** the other person to seek reconciliation. So many people have the roots of bitterness deeply embedded in their souls because of the poison of unforgiveness. When we forgive, we open the opportunity for others to be treated in a way that they may never have been exposed to before. I believe one of the most important measures of servant leadership is a person's willingness, humility, and openness in regard to forgiveness of others, no matter how others have treated them or hurt them. **Forgiveness is a choice!** Learn to ask for and give forgiveness; reflect and be mindful of how you have been blessed and forgiven in so many areas of your life. When you lose sight of how much you have to be thankful for, you will always be justified in your own spirit to hold a grudge or withhold forgiveness.

Two Practical Tools to Help with Difficult Conversations

In working with leaders over the years, I have found that we need practical tools and skills to reinforce both common sense and common actions. I personally need a simple way of approaching the most difficult and hard things of life. In our servant leadership training sessions, we have introduced two such simple tools that have been extremely helpful in navigating the rough waters of having difficult healthy conversations.

Four-Part Apology Tool

At the heart of servant leadership is the foundational and essential building block of relationships. As we have established throughout this book, relationships are key to our ability to serve and lead. Too often, either because of pride or fear, we don't acknowledge our part in conflict. An apology is not just a social nicety. It is an important way of showing respect and empathy for the wronged person. It is also a way of acknowledging an act that, if otherwise left unnoticed, might compromise the relationship. An apology has the ability to disarm others of their anger and to prevent further misunderstandings. Although an apology cannot undo harmful past actions, if done sincerely and effectively, it can undo the negative effects of those actions.

Following are the four parts of the apology tool with a scenario of taking responsibility for not finishing a report on time. Notice that the ownership for the behavior and actions is taken by the person apologizing and asking forgiveness.

1. **Acknowledge:** "I didn't get the report finished."
2. **Apologize**: "I apologize for not meeting expectations." **(Never use the word *sorry*.)**
3. **Make it right**: "What can I do to make it right?" **(A logical consequence)**
4. **Recommit:** "In the future, I will get assignments completed when asked." **(Always state this in the positive—e.g., not "I won't forget to get my report in on time.")**

A senior executive talked about using the four-part apology:

> *One time I vented my frustrations with a sharp tongue onto a direct report who informed me of additional costs regarding a project we were working on. Nothing pushes my buttons more than being caught off guard by the unexpected. Ten minutes later, at a restaurant, my thinking kicked in. The only honorable thing to do was to go back and apologize. When she saw me coming toward her desk, she surely thought, "Oh no. Not him." She braced herself when I approached. "I came back to apologize to you. You didn't deserve the negative stuff I dished out, and I sincerely apologize for affecting you." At first she looked at me with disbelief. Then she extended her hand toward me. "Thank you," she said slowly and sincerely. "No one has ever done that before." I didn't even get to finish the*

> *four parts, but I did tell her that, in the future, I will not blame or point the finger when I hear unexpected bad news.*[59]

A team leader confessed how she hated conflict; the fear was deeply rooted in her background, and the thought of going to a person to ask forgiveness was stressful and frightening to her.

> *I hate conflict, and I guess I just internalize or stuff it. What I have realized is that my avoidance has only caused me and others more pain. To be honest, when you talked about the four-part apology, the first person I thought of was my husband. I need to ask his forgiveness for how I have been treating him and holding on to grudges. I have become bitter, and my attitude is ruining our marriage. I made the decision right there and then to take action, and after much worry and stress over something I found so simple, I talked with my husband and used the format of the four-part apology. I have to admit that I just it read it to him, but as I did, tears welled up in his eyes, and he said, "I love you." I have taken a big step in my life, but most of all in healing our marriage. Thank you for encouraging me to take this giant leap forward.*[60]

A school leader expressed that he thought and to some extent was taught that admitting fault or wrong was a sign of weakness:

> *I know that this sounds strange, but I believed and was taught that I should never show weakness and that admitting to fault or wrong is a sign that leaders are weak. Even as I write this, I feel stupid for thinking like that, but I did. Hey, I just admitted to a fault. As you can guess, apologies make me uncomfortable. However, I took the challenge, and the person I needed to apologize to was my oldest son. I realized I never admitted any wrongdoing to him, and it made me think about what kind of example am I being to him. My macho thinking was destroying my relationship with him. I am so thankful because I took the first step in repairing my relationship with my son. I asked his forgiveness for my behavior and never admitting fault. I broke down in tears, and he hugged me. I guess when you are weak, then you are really strong.*[61]

The "I" Message Tool

The point of an "I-message" is to express our own feelings directly, clearly, and without accusation. Using this kind of approach appeals to the heart and conscience of another and allows the other individual to make choices. The model, which works especially well with teens, includes five critical parts:

I care, I see, I feel, I need, and I will

I Care: We begin by letting people know that we care about them. This not only motivates them to listen, but more importantly, it reminds us how important they are to us, and that we don't wish to hurt or attack them. Here are some examples of the "I care" element of an I-message: "Cindy, you are someone I trust, and you are very important to me." "I care about you, John, very much." "Mary, I value our friendship and care about you and our relationship." "Pete, I believe in you and want the very best for you."

I See: Next, we describe the specific behavior that has triggered our feelings. This is the "I see" element. This isn't an opinion or a judgment; it is just a specific description of a behavior. Here are some examples of this element: "When you wait and don't tell me bad news until it is after the fact…" "When you talk about the issue with other people but avoid telling me…" "You are not following through on agreed expectations." "Your tone and body language tell me that something is bothering you."

Feel: In the third part, we express our feelings directly. Again, this isn't an opinion or a judgment—just a statement of feeling. It's important to use a feeling word here, such as *mad, sad, happy, hurt, ashamed, afraid,* and so forth. It is also important to not follow the word *feel* with words such as *that* or *like*. In that case, we are not stating a feeling but a thought or opinion. This is usually a veiled judgment. "I feel that you are being inconsiderate" includes no feeling word and really means that we are judging someone's behavior. Here are some examples of the "I feel" element: "I feel scared and angry." "I feel hurt." "When you avoid telling important information, it makes me mad." "Your actions and behavior make me feel unappreciated and devalued."

I Need: This is followed by letting the other person know what we need from him or her. This statement clearly expresses our own need in the relationship without shaming or blaming the other person. It should be a very specific statement. Here are some examples of the "I need" element: "I need you to call if you are going to be late, no matter what the reason." "I need you to tell me bad news no matter what the circumstance." "I need you to be more willing to ask for my help." "I need you to follow through on your commitments."

I Will: Finally, the statement concludes with the "I will" element, which is simply your commitment to the other person. This statement allows the other person to know specifically what you will do in the future. It is not intended to be used as a threat, but it may state logical consequences or next steps if the behavior or issue isn't addressed. Here are some examples of the "I will" element: "I will listen to your explanation and take it into account." "If you've called in advance when something unforeseen occurs, I will not automatically dock you if you're late." "I will not overreact when you present bad news." "I will be open to listen and not judge or criticize." In this manner, we can express our intentions directly and clearly, without lecturing or attacking.

The point is simple. The reason we need to express our feelings is to model healthy behavior, respect, care, and appropriate ways to deal with conflict or disagreement. In addition, our own needs as a servant leader need to be addressed through the setting of an intimate relationship. Expressing our feelings should not be used to shame or guilt the others into new behavior. We don't tell others we feel hurt by their behavior so that they will apologize. We do it so they can experience a model of how to express feelings in a direct and respectful manner, and we do it so that we don't harbor hurt, anger, resentment, or bitterness toward them, resulting in inappropriate reactions and behaviors on our part.

I have made mistakes, I have done so many things the wrong way, and I have inappropriately handled myself both personally and professionally. But with all that I have done wrong, there are things I know I have done right: I've made myself vulnerable to others, admitted my wrongs, and been open with them when they hurt me. This is an especially important concept for men. I believe that when we communicate this way, others learn that it's perfectly normal and natural for a man to admit weakness and to feel hurt. There are too many men who have a false concept of manhood and misunderstand the power of personal humility and authenticity. Men confuse manhood with "macho" and refuse to say they're sorry or to show hurt or weakness because if you do, then you are not a "real" man. The lie of the "macho" man has caused more pain, hurt, and tragedy in our children than just about any other lie that has been fostered in the world. The real strength of a man comes when he is able to humbly and with great personal strength model how to deal with inappropriate behavior, sin, or wrongs in an appropriate, honest, and controlled manner.

The I-message format is a tool to help servant leaders to communicate with others. It may seem at first a little too artificial or cumbersome to follow. The key is to understand that the tool is just a means to help you communicate your heart. It may seem unnatural or awkward, but over time, you may find it to be an effective tool of communication.

An HR recruiter shared how she avoided difficult conversations that involved her personally even though as part of her job, she had difficult conversations all of the time:

> *I hate conflict, and I know you would never guess it because of my job in HR. As a result of the training and being exposed to the tools on having difficult conversations, it made me realize that on the personal side and at times professional if it involves me, I avoid conflict at any cost. When you challenged us with thinking of a difficult conversation you need have but haven't yet had, I immediately knew the conversation I needed to have. The I-message format gave me a way to write down my thoughts*

and organize how I was going to approach that conversation. I have to say, I was very nervous about having that conversation, but sticking to the format gave me courage, and overall the conversation went well. In fact, I was able to communicate clearly, for the first time, what was really impacting me at work and my performance.[62]

A senior-level leader expressed how he used the I-message format to have a difficult conversation with his son, who is in his early twenties:

Usually, I just wing it when it comes to talking to my children. However, I have found that I do a lot of talking and not much listening. The I-message format allowed me to have a difficult conversation with my son about a major life and career decision he was trying to make. It allowed me to express my feelings at a level that I had never really openly expressed with him. When I shared that I was hurt by how he was behaving and proceeding without any consideration for me or his mother, he stopped being defensive and was visibly shaken. He had tears in his eyes and expressed that he had never heard me talk like this before. All I can say is that one conversation is building a whole new foundation for how we are going to interact from this point forward.[63]

A high school administrator stated that she needed to have a difficult conversation with a teacher whom she was evaluating, but because of past history, she had been avoiding and basically allowing that teacher to get away with "bad" behavior:

I knew immediately when you challenged us with having difficult conversations that I needed to step up and have this conversation with a bully of a teacher. Admittedly, I had been avoiding this conversation because I just didn't want the stress and conflict that comes with dealing with her. Following the I-message format lowered my stress level, and especially taking the time to write down what was the main issue that I saw. It also helped me to take down the emotional level that was hindering me from having the strength and courage to confront the teacher in a healthy way. I knew along that I needed to have the conversation, but I honestly just didn't have the right mind-set or tools. Thank you, because even though the teacher didn't initially receive what I had to say to her, over the past couple of weeks, I noticed a significant change in the way she interacts with and treats people.[64]

The hands of a servant leader are committed to taking action. It is your **responsibility** and your **privilege** to be the person who helps people get better. That often begins with a candid conversation. I believe that people can improve their attitudes and their abilities. And, as mentioned, because I do, I talk to them about where they're coming up short. If you're a leader, and you want to help serve people, you need to be willing to have those difficult conversations.

Question for Reflection

In our servant leadership training sessions, we challenge people with having healthy conflict through difficult conversations. The challenge is simple: *What difficult conversation do you know you need to have and haven't yet had?*

Considering this question, in the next thirty to sixty days, who will you have that difficult conversation with, and when will you have it?

You have principles and tools that can effectively help you in having a difficult conversation. **Take action now!**

Epilogue

> *We know that leadership is very much related to change. As the pace of change accelerates, there is naturally a greater need for effective leadership.*
> —John Kotter, *Leading Change*

This book has been a journey into the ***heart, head, and hands of a servant leader***. As John Maxwell has said, "Everything rises and falls on leadership." The question is not one of whether you are a leader; rather, it is a question of how you will lead. All of us lead, whether we are conscious of it or not, intentional or not, purposeful or not. We all will have an influence, and the underlying question that this book highlights is as follows: **What kind of influence will it be?** We all have influence, but what choices can you make today that will create and cultivate a better future and leave a positive impact on your sphere of influence?

Leading is doing! Twelve frogs are sitting on a log, and one decides to jump. How many frogs are still remaining on the log? What is your answer? The correct answer is twelve! That's right—it isn't a trick question. Why? Because the one frog only decided to jump; the frog didn't actually take the leap. There is an enormous difference between deciding and doing. The same is true for servant leadership. Learning about leadership and being a servant leader is not the same as leading by serving. Deciding to be an exemplary leader and a person of character and integrity is not the same as actually being one. Leading is doing, and you have to take action to be a servant leader. You need to make the heart, head, and hands of a servant leader a daily habit. You need to do something every day to learn more and to take action on what you know. You need to jump into the pond, demonstrate that you know how to stay afloat, and over time, like the frog, become a more capable swimmer in the pond of life.

Every day we have an opportunity to make a small difference. I could coach someone better, I could listen better, I could ask better questions, I could be more positive, I could say "thank you" more, I could be more intentional about giving praise and appreciation, I could choose to engage in healthy conversations, I could love others more...and the list goes on.

Making progress every day is not easy; stuff happens that can seriously disrupt you. But the goal remains to find ways to make meaningful progress every day. How do you do this? Big wins are great, but they rarely happen. Thinking only of major wins is like baseball players who are always swinging for the fences, trying to hit a homerun. They don't usually have the best batting averages. The good news is that small wins every day boost your inner life tremendously. Just getting on base and doing it consistently is going to boost your batting average. With that in mind, just doing something every day, with minor steps forward, will give you the confidence and hope to keep moving forward. You have the opportunity every day to serve. To serve is to lead!

This book was written with you in mind. You have unique value and greatness, and only you can serve your "sweet spot" to the world. You can make a difference. You can choose today to adopt the heart, head, and hands of a servant leader.

As we have seen, genius is found in simplicity! Over two thousand years ago, a young Jewish rabbi introduced a radical concept of leadership. His philosophy not only defied the leadership understanding of His day, but it also continues to challenge the leadership thinking of contemporary theorists and practitioners. Jesus answers the **"missing link" of leadership**. A leader is first and foremost a servant of the people. Who, then, is a leader? Anyone and everyone who is willing to serve! Anyone who is willing and daring enough to care for others.

How about you? Are you willing to serve? Are you willing to take action from your head, heart, and hands? Are you a man or woman who dares to care? Will you join the Master's way to unleash personal greatness to serve others? The choice is yours!

ENDNOTES

1. Myles Munroe, *The Spirit of Leadership* (New Kensington, PA: Whitaker House, 2005), 13.

2. Bill O'Reilly and Martin Dugard, *Killing Jesus: A History* (New York: Holt, 2013), 3.

3. Myles Munroe, *In Charge* (New York: FaithWords, 2008), 118.

4. "5 Leadership Lessons: EntreLeadership," Michael McKinley, *Leading Now* (blog), October 14, 2011, http://www.leadershipnow.com/leadingblog/2011/10/5_leadership_lessons_entrelead.html.

5. "What Is Servant Leadership?" Greenleaf Center of Servant Leadership, (cites Greenleaf's 1970 "The Servant as Leader" essay), https://www.greenleaf.org/what-is-servant-leadership.

6. "Servant Leaders Company List," Modern Servant Leader, (cites *Fortune* magazine's annual list "100 Best Companies to Work For" for 2015 and lists servant leadership companies), July 26, 2015, http://modernservantleader.com/featured/servant-leadership-companies-list.

7. Munroe, *The Spirit of Leadership*, 177.

8. Caroline Leaf, *Who Switched Off My Brain?* (Southlake, TX: Inprov, 2009), 19–20.

9. Munroe, *In Charge* (New York: FaithWords, 2008), 100.

10. Matthew 20:25–28 NASB.

11. Myles Munroe, *Understanding Your Potential* (Shippensburg, PA: Destiny Image, 2005), 15.

12. Ralph Waldo Trine, *In Tune with the Infinite* (New York: Penguin, 1897, 2008), 6.

13. Carol Dweck, *Mindset* (New York: Ballantine, 2006), 16.

14. Warren Bennis, *On Becoming a Leader* (New York: Addison-Wesley, 1994), 56.

15. Ibid., 56–57.

16. John G. Miller, *Flipping the Switch* (New York: Putnam, 2006), 8.

17. John Maxwell, *Failing Forward* (Nashville: Thomas Nelson, 2000), 2.

18. Bennis, *On Becoming a Leader*, 68–69.

19. Daniel Goleman, *Focus: The Hidden Driver of Excellence* (New York: Harper, 2013), 4.

20. John Maxwell, *21 Indispensable Qualities of a Leader* (Nashville: Thomas Nelson, 1998), 180.

21. "Please Respect My Time: Dealing with People Who Are Always Late," Dr. F. M. Forni, as quoted in Professor's House's article, no publication date listed, http://www.professorshouse.com/relationships/general/articles/please-respect-my-time.

22. "10 Ways You're Wasting Other People's Time," Craig Jarrow, *Time Management Ninja* (blog), October 3, 2013, https://timemanagementninja.com/2013/03/10.

23. "Selflessness," Doug Moran, *If You Will Lead* (blog), May 24, 2016, http://www.ifyouwilllead.com/the-if-16-leadership-attributes-4-selflessness.

24. Bob Burg and John Mann, *The Go-Giver: A Little Story about a Powerful Business Idea* (New York: Penguin 2007, 2015), 63.

25. Ibid, 123.

26. Myles Munroe, *The Power of Character in Leadership* (New Kensington, PA: Whitaker House, 2014), 192–193.

27. "The 10 Attributes of Trustworthy People," Carl A. Osborne, *DVM360 Magazine,* January 15, 2005, http://veterinarynews.dvm360.com/10-attributes-trustworthy-people?id=&sk=&date=&pageID=2.

28. "The Leadership Challenge: How to Make Extraordinary Things Happen in Organizations," James Kouzes and Barry Posner, *Audio-Tech Business Book Summaries,* August 2008, http://audiotech.com.

29. Ibid.

30. "Do You Have the Courage to Be Honest?" Jonathan Wells, *Advanced Life Skills* (web series blog), January 2016, http://advancedlifeskills.com/blog/courage-to-be-honest.

31. Leaf, *Who Switched Off My Brain,* 15.

32. Ibid, 40.

33. Ibid, 43.

34. Goleman, *Focus,* 210.

35. Henry Cloud, *Boundaries for Leaders: Results, Relationships, and Being Ridiculously in Charge* (New York: HarperCollins, 2013), 27.

36. Servant Leadership Coaching System Sixty-Day Challenge 2016 testimonies, permission given by participants, 1.

37. Ibid, testimonies, 2.

38. Ibid, testimonies, 3.

39. Goleman, *Focus*, 69.

40. Servant Leadership Coaching System 60 Day Challenge 2016 testimonies, permission given by participants.

41. Cloud, *Boundaries for Leaders*, 103–112.

42. Roger Connors and Tom Smith, *The Oz Principle: Getting Results Through Individual and Organizational Accountability* (New York: Penguin, 2004), 10–11.

43. Cloud, *Boundaries for Leaders*, 111.

44. Leaf, *Who Switched Off My Brain?* 46.

45. Cloud, *Boundaries for Leaders*, 140–145.

46. Servant Leadership Coaching System 60 Day Challenge 2016 testimonies, permission given by participants, 4.

47. Ibid, testimonies, 4.

48. Ibid, testimonies. 5.

49. Ibid, testimonies, 6.

50. Norm Doidge, *The Brain That Changes Itself* (New York: Penguin, 2007), xix-xx.

51. Jeffery M. Schwartz, Henry P. Stapp, and Mario Beauregard, "Quantum Physics in Neuroscience and Psychology: A Neurophysical Model of Mind–Brain Interaction," *Philological Transactions of the Royal Society*, doi:10.1098/rstb.2004.1598 (2004): 12.

52. Leaf, *Who Switched Off My Brain?* 46.

53. Servant Leadership Coaching System 60 Day Challenge 2016 testimonies, permission given by participants, 7.

54. Ibid, testimonies, 8.

55. Ibid, testimonies, 9.

56. Matthew D. Lieberman, *Social: Why Our Brains Are Wired to Connect* (New York: Crown, 2013), 43.

57. Ibid, 64.

58. George Kohlrieser, Susan Goldsworthy, and Duncan Coombe, *Care to Dare: Unleashing Astonishing Potential through Secure Base Leadership* (San Francisco, CA: Jossey-Bass, 2012), 212–214.

59. Servant Leadership Coaching System 60 Day Challenge 2016 testimonies, permission given by participants, 10.

60. Ibid, testimonies, 11.

61. Ibid, testimonies, 12.

62. Ibid, testimonies, 13.

63. Ibid, testimonies, 14.

64. Ibid, testimonies, 15.

REFERENCES

Assaraf, J., and M. Smith. *The Answer: Grow Any Business, Achieve Financial Freedom, and Live an Extraordinary Life.* New York: Atria Books, Simon & Schuster, 2008.

Autry, J. *The Servant Leader.* New York: Three Rivers Press, 2001.

Bennis, W. *On Becoming a Leader.* New York: Addison-Wesley, 1994.

Brady, C., and Woodward. *Launching a Leadership Revolution.* Grand Blanc, MI: Obstacles Press, 2005.

Burg, B., and J. Mann. *The Go-Giver: A Little Story about a Powerful Business Idea.* New York: Penguin Press, 2007, 2015.

Cloud, H. *Boundaries for Leaders: Results, Relationships, and Being Ridiculously in Charge.* New York: Harper-Collins, 2013.

Collins, J. *Good to Great.* New York: Harper Business, 2001.

Conners, R., T. Smith, and C. Hickman. *The Oz Principle: Getting Results through Individual and Organizational Accountability.* New York: Penguin Group, 2004.

Covey, S. *The Seven Habits of Highly Effective People.* New York: Simon and Schuster, 1989.

Covey, S. *Principle Centered Leadership.* New York: Random House, 1991.

Covey, S. *The 8th Habit: From Effectiveness to Greatness.* New York: Simon and Schuster, 2004.

Covey, S. M. R. *The Speed of Trust: The One Thing That Changes Everything.* New York: Simon and Schuster, 2006.

De Pree, M. *Leadership Is an Art.* New York: Doubleday, 1988.

De Pree, M. *Leading without Power.* San Francisco, CA: Jossey-Bass, 1997.

Doidge, N. *The Brain That Changes Itself: Stories of Personal Triumph from the Frontiers of Brain Science.* New York: Penguin Books, 2007.

Doidge, N. *The Brain's Way of Healing: Remarkable Discoveries from the Frontiers of Neuroplasticity.* New York: Viking Press, 2015.

Duhigg, C. *The Power of Habit: Why We Do What We Do in Life and Business.* New York: Random House, 2012.

Edmondson, A. "The Competitive Imperative of Learning." *Harvard Business Review* (July–August 2008), 60–67.

Finzel, Hans, *The Top Ten Mistakes Leaders Make.* Colorado Springs, CO: David C. Cook, 2007.

Glaser, J. E. *The DNA of Leadership: Leverage Your Instincts to Communicate, Differentiate, Innovate.* Avon, MA: Platinum Press, 2006.

Glaser, J. E. *Conversational Intelligence: How Great Leaders Build Trust and Get Extraordinary Results.* Brookline, MA: Bibliomotion, 2014.

Goleman, D. *Focus: The Hidden Driver of Excellence.* New York: Harper-Collins, 2013.

Goleman, D., and R. Boyatzis. "Social Intelligence and the Biology of Leadership." *Harvard Business Review* (September 2008), 74–81.

Gordan, E. "NeuroLeadership and Integrative Neuroscience: 'It's about Validation Stupid!'" *NeuroLeadership Journal* 1 (2008), 71–80.

Greenleaf, R. K. *Servant Leadership: A Journey into the Nature of Legitimate Power and Greatness.* New York: Paulist Press, 1977.

Hassed, C. "Mindfulness, Well-Being and Performance." *NeuroLeadership Journal* 1 (2008), 53–60.

Irving, J.A., G. J. Longbotham. "Team Effectiveness and Six Essential Servant Leadership Themes: A Regression Model Based on Items in the Organizational Leadership Assessment." *International Journal of Leadership Studies* 2, no. 2 (2007), 98–113.

Jensen, R. Achieving *Authentic Success*. San Francisco, CA: Life Coach Foundation, 2001.

Jung-Beeman, M., A. Collier, and J. Kounios. "How Insight Happens: Learning from the Brain." *NeuroLeadership Journal* 1 (2008), 20–25.

Kohlrieser, G., S. Goldsmith, and D. Coombe. *Care to Dare: Unleashing Astonishing Potential through Secure Base Leadership*. New York: John Wiley & Sons, 2012.

Kotter, J. *Leading Change*. Boston, MA: HBS Press, 1996.

Kotter, J. *What Leaders Really Do*. Boston, MA: HBS Press, 1999.

Kotter, J. *The Heart of Change*. Boston, MA: HBS Press, 2002.

Kouzes, J., and B. Posner. *The Leadership Challenge: How to Make Extraordinary Things Happen in Organizations*. San Francisco, CA: Jossey-Bass, 1998.

Kriegel, R., and D. Brandt. *Sacred Cows Make the Best Burgers: Developing Change Ready People and Organizations*. New York: Warner Books, 1996.

Leaf, C. *Who Switched Off My Brain? Controlling Toxic Thoughts and Emotions*, Southlake, TX: Inprov Ltd., 2009.

Lencioni, P. *The Five Dysfunctions of a Team*. San Francisco, CA: Jossey-Bass, 2002.

Lencioni, P. *The Advantage: Why Organizational Health Trumps Everything Else in Business.* San Francisco, CA: Jossey-Bass, 2012.

Lieberman, M. *Social: Why Our Brains Are Wired to Connect.* New York: Crown Publishers, 2013.

Lieberman, M., and N. Eisenberger. "The Pains and Pleasures of Social Life: A Social Cognitive Neuroscience Approach." *NeuroLeadership Journal* 1 (2008), 38–43.

Ochsner, K. "Staying Cool under Pressure: Insights from Social Cognitive Neuroscience and Their Implications for Self and Society." *NeuroLeadership Journal* 1 (2008), 26–32. 2008.

O'Reilly, B., and M. Dugard. *Killing Jesus: A History.* New York: Holt Publishers, 2013.

Maxwell, J. *Developing the Leader within You.* Nashville, TN: Thomas Nelson, 1993.

Maxwell, J. *Failing Forward.* Nashville, TN: Thomas Nelson, 1999.

Maxwell, J. *21 Irrefutable Laws of Leadership.* Nashville, TN: Thomas Nelson, 2000.

Maxwell, J. *Think for a Change.* New York: Warner Business Books, 2003.

Miller, J. *QBQ! The Question behind the Question: What to Really Ask Yourself about Practicing Personal Accountability.* Denver, CO: Denver Press, 2001.

Miller, J. *Flipping the Switch: Unleashing the Power of Personal Accountability Using QBQ.* New York: Putnam Press, 2006.

Modern Servant Leader. "Servant Leaders Company List." July 26, 2015. http://modernservantleader.com/featured/servant-leadership-companies-list.

Munroe, M. *The Spirit of Leadership: Cultivating the Attitudes That Influence Human Action.* New Kensington, PA: Whitaker House, 2005.

Munroe, M. *Understanding Your Potential: Discovering the Hidden You.* Shippensburg, PA: Destiny Image, 2005.

Munroe, M. *In Charge: Finding the Leader within You.* New York: FaithWords, 2008.

Munroe, M. *Becoming a Leader: Discovering the Leader You Were Meant to Be!* New Kensington, PA: Whitaker House, 2009.

Munroe, M. *The Power of Character in Leadership: How Values, Morals, Ethics, and Principles Affect Leaders.* New Kensington, PA: Whitaker House, 2014.

Ramsey, D. *EntreLeadership: 20 Years of Practical Business Wisdom from the Trenches.* New York: Howard Books, 2011.

Rath, T. *Are You Fully Charged? 3 Keys to Energizing Your Work and Life.* San Francisco, CA: Silicon Guild, 2015.

Rath, T., and D. Clifton. *How Full Is Your Bucket?* New York: Gallup Press, 2004.

Ringleb, A. H., and D. Rock. "The Emerging Field of NeuroLeadership." *NeuroLeadership Journal* 1 (2008), 3–19.

Rock, D. *Quiet Leadership: Six Steps to Transforming Performance at Work.* New York: Harper-Collins, 2006.

Rock, D. "SCARF: A Brain-Based Model for Collaborating with and Influencing Others." *NeuroLeadership Journal* 1 (2008), 44–52.

Rock, D., and J. Schwartz. "The Neuroscience of Leadership. Breakthroughs in Brain Research Explain How to Make Organizational Transformation Succeed." *Strategy + Business*, 2006, http://www.strategy-business.com/article/062007.

Rubin, G. *Better than Before: Mastering Habits of Our Everyday Lives.* New York: Crown Publishers, 2015.

Schwartz, J. *Brain Lock: A Four-Step Self-Treatment Method to Change Your Brain Chemistry.* New York: Harper-Collins, 1996.

Schwartz, J., and S. Begley. *The Mind and the Brain: Neuroplasticity and the Power of Mental Force.* New York: Harper-Collins, 2002.

Schwartz, J., and R. Gladding, *You Are Not Your Brain: The 4-Step Solution for Changing Bad Habits, Ending Unhealthy Thinking, and Taking Control of Your Life.* New York: Penguin Group, 2011.

Senge, P. *The Fifth Discipline: The Art and Practice of the Learning Organization.* New York: Doubleday-Currency, 1990.

Senge, P. *The Dance of Change: The Challenges of Sustaining Momentum in Learning Organizations.* New York: Doubleday-Currency, 1999.

Stabile, M. *The Servant Leadership Coaching System's: 60-Day Challenge Testimonials,* unpublished testimonials with permission from participants, FutureNow Consulting, LLC, 2016.

Tang, Y., and M. Posner. "The Neuroscience of Mindfulness." *NeuroLeadership Journal* 1 (2008), 33–37.

Trine, R. W. *In Tune with the Infinite.* New York: Tarcher/Penguin, 1897, 2007.

Waters, L. "Using Human Brain Dynamics to Enhance Workplace Team Dynamics: Evidence from Two Applied Case Studies." *NeuroLeadership Journal* 1 (2008), 61–66.

Wells, J. "Do You Have the Courage to Be Honest?" (blog), *Advanced Life Skills*, http://advancedlifeskills.com/blog/courage-to-be-honest/.

About the Author

Michael J. Stabile, PhD, uses his extensive leadership training in a wide variety of vocations: education, leadership and life coaching, consulting, and writing. But the same theme permeates his many positions of influence: he is passionate about inspiring and empowering others to be change agents in their homes, jobs, and communities.

Mike's company, FutureNow Consulting LLC, uses workshops, seminars, and customized life coaching to effect transformational change at the individual, group, and organizational levels.

Mike and his wife, Pam, live in Cincinnati, Ohio. They are blessed with three married daughters and six grandchildren.

Mike's leadership writing extends beyond nonfiction: you can find the fictional *Papa's Legacy: A Leadership Parable* on amazon.com and other retail outlets.

If you are interested in contacting Mike for workshops, keynote speaking, or a presentation based upon concepts presented in this book, contact him at mstabile@futurenowed.com *or visit his website for additional workshop information or services of FutureNow Consulting, LLC, at* www.futurenowed.com.

Made in the USA
Middletown, DE
17 March 2018